P9-DDX-555

THREE SWAHILI
WOMEN

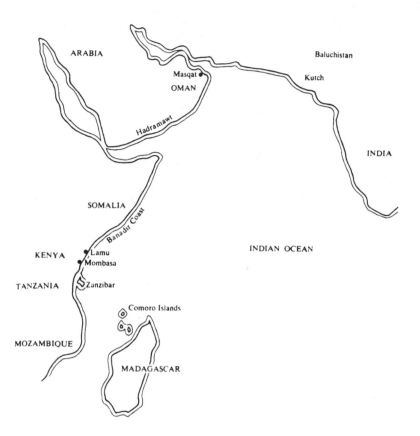

Map 1. The Indian Ocean

THREE SWAHILI WOMEN

LIFE HISTORIES FROM MOMBASA, KENYA

EDITED AND TRANSLATED BY

Sarah Mirza and Margaret Strobel

Indiana University Press
Bloomington & Indianapolis

Copyright © 1989 by Margaret Strobel

All rights reserved

No part of this book may be reproduced or utilized in any form or by any means, electronic or mechanical, including photocopying and recording, or by any information storage and retrieval system, without permission in writing from the publisher. The Association of American University Presses' Resolution on Permissions constitutes the only exception to this prohibition.

Manufactured in the United States of America

Library of Congress Cataloging-in-Publication Data

Wanawake Watatu Waswahili wa Mombasa, Kenya. English.
    Three Swahili Women: Life Histories from Mombasa, Kenya.

    Translation of: Wanawake Waswahili Watatu wa Mombasa, Kenya.
    Bibliography: p.
    Includes index.
    1. Women--Kenya--Mombasa--History. 2. Women, Muslim--Kenya--Mombasa--Biography. 3. Sociology--Biographical methods. I. Mirza, Sarah, 1951-   . II. Strobel, Margaret, 1946- . III. Title.
HQ1796.5.W3613 1989   305.4'2'0967623   88-45093
ISBN 0-253-36012-9
ISBN 0-253-28854-1 (pbk.)

1 2 3 4 5 93 92 91 90 89

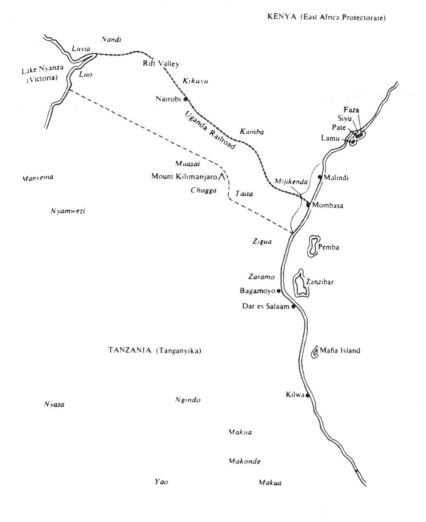

Map 2.   East Africa

Note: Names of peoples are in italics.

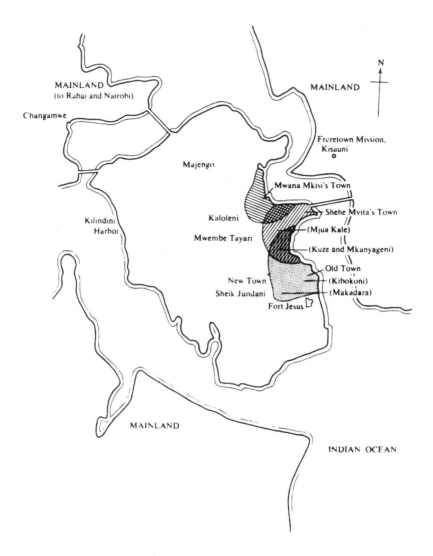

Map 3.   Mombasa

CONTENTS

PREFACE

This collection of life histories evolved as a joint project of Sarah Mirza and Margaret Strobel over a period of several years. The doctoral dissertation research of which these interviews were a part in 1972-1973 and 1975 was funded by a Fulbright-Hays Doctoral Dissertation Abroad grant and a Woodrow Wilson Doctoral Dissertation Fellowship in Women's Studies. The Campus Research Board of the University of Illinois at Chicago funded two trips by Margaret Strobel to Los Angeles to confer with Sarah Mirza. The Office of Social Science Research at UIC provided word processing for most of the English text. The manuscript was completed during Margaret Strobel's tenure as a Fellow of the Institute for the Humanities at the University of Illinois at Chicago. Evelyn Okanya typed the Swahili texts. Special thanks are due to Joan Hoff-Wilson, who had the Swahili typescript scanned onto a computer disk, saving much time and innumerable errors in the separately published Swahili volume.[1] We also wish to thank the Kenya National Archives for assistance in the research that contributed to the introductions to each chapter. Yale University Press graciously agreed to allow us to use the maps from Margaret Strobel's *Muslim Women in Mombasa, 1890-1975*.[2]

The greatest thanks must go to Kaje wa Mwenye Matano, Mishi wa Abdala, and Shamsa Muhamad Muhashamy for consenting to the project and thereby providing us with hours of fun (and some drudgery). Several people transcribed tapes, including Sarah's siblings Nazarat and Arzein (before the collaboration began) and others. The family of the now deceased Abusuleiman Mazrui introduced

Strobel to Kaje wa Mwenye Matano and Shamsa Muhamad Muhashamy and acted as a surrogate family during her stay in Mombasa. When Mirza returned to Mombasa in November 1985, Mishi wa Abdala's granddaughter Rukia helped communicate with her grandmother, who had memory lapses. Sulafa Mazrui assisted in innumerable ways. We greatly appreciate the critical comments of Edward A. Alpers, Frederick Cooper, Susan Geiger, Fatma Husein, Claire Robertson, Mary Shirimo, Zubeida Tumbo-Masabo, Karen Tranberg Hansen, and Marcia Wright. Sharifa Zawawi carefully checked both the Swahili and the translation. The errors that remain are, of course, our responsibility. We did not always follow their (sometimes contradictory) advice, but we received many useful comments for reorganization, editing, and improved translation. Finally, we thank our editor Joan Catapano for convincing Indiana University Press to publish a bilingual edition and for her help generally with the project.

Mirza and Strobel believe that these life histories will be interesting and useful in a variety of contexts. Since there is little Swahili literature about women, these texts can provide a Swahili-speaking audience with an understanding of the private and public activities of females. Used with the English translations, the texts offer Swahili language students examples of actual spoken language, a rarity in language-learning materials. (Because of degrees of difficulty, we suggest that language students read the life histories in reverse order.) Linguists will find the presentation of Kimvita (Mombasa dialect) from women of different ages and social contexts instructive. Finally, an English-speaking audience can use the translations to understand, in this particular society, the roles of women and the relationship between an individual and her society and to compare these cross-culturally with those of women around the world.

Any project that extends over such a long period of time has its ups and downs, its periods of exhilaration and despair. This one has been squeezed in between the jobs of Sarah Mirza at the Kenya Tourist Office in Los Angeles and Margaret Strobel at the Women's Studies Program at the University of Illinois at Chicago. It was also squeezed into the latter's maternity leave, so that three-week-old and colicky Jessica was soothed by listening to Swahili lullabies

and taped interviews.   Margaret Strobel would also like to
thank her husband, Bill Barclay, for his support through all
this, in the face of his firm belief that it would never reach
completion.

Los Angeles
Chicago

GLOSSARY

The following Swahili words appear frequently in the English text. Swahili nouns usually consist of a root and prefix. Singular words are made plural by changing the prefix (plural forms are in parentheses).

beni: Swahili brass band (also gwaride, bwaride)
buibui: black robe worn by Muslim women on the Swahili coast
bwaride: Swahili brass band (also gwaride, beni)
gwaride: Swahili brass band (also bwaride, beni)
kanga: leso; two cloths worn by women
kungwi (makungwi; abstract form, ukungwi): woman who initiates girls at puberty
lelemama: a dance style brought to Mombasa from Zanzibar; popular especially between the world wars
leso: kanga; two pieces of printed cloth; a major item of clothing, especially among more traditional women, and ritual exchange
madrasa: religious class
mila: customary practice
mmiji (wamiji): female elder(s) of the Twelve Tribes
mwaadhini: person who sounds the call to prayer in the mosque
mzalia (wazalia): a locally born, not an imported, slave; person of slave ancestry
sharifu (masharifu): reputed descendant of the Prophet
sheria: Islamic law
somo: a woman who instructs girls in menstrual and sexual matters
utani: traditional link between Mijikenda and the Twelve Tribes

THREE SWAHILI
WOMEN

Introduction

Life Histories

Life histories offer the opportunity to observe a particular society through the lens of individual lives. Unlike autobiographies, the initiation for which generally comes from the subject herself, a life history comes about as the collaboration between two individuals, often an insider speaking about herself and her society and an outsider asking questions from her own frame of reference.[1] As such, a life history from the start embodies more than one person's agenda, purpose, and interests.

Paradoxically, the agenda of the collector of the narrative (which may become modified in interaction with the narrator) is often easier to discern than that of the narrator herself. In Africa, missionaries are an early source of life histories, which have subsequently been reproduced and reinterpreted by historians. Often the intent of these life stories of African converts was to show the tribulations and successes of doing "the Lord's work." Yet in the hands of skilled scholars, these stories yield important insights about individuals, societies, and historical processes of change. Marcia Wright has analyzed the life stories of three women who experienced slavery and the slave trade in nineteenth-century east-central Africa.[2] The stories of two of the women, Narwimba and Chisi, were collected by a Moravian missionary. The third, Meli, dictated her story to her son for publication. Wright utilizes the three to give a sense of the variety of individual responses to the exceedingly disruptive period of the slave trade and to highlight the impact of gender on one's options and experience.

Another example of this type of source is presented by Edward Alpers, who examines the life of Swema, a ten-year-old Yao girl captured around 1865 in east Africa.[3] Although the missionary recorder of Swema's tale appears to have more explicit intentions to use her life as a Christian example, her story vividly portrays the experience of the slave caravan.

The explicitly historical use of personal narratives contrasts with the more common anthropological perspective of classical texts documenting the lives of African women. An early, and until recently unmatched, example of this genre is Mary F. Smith's *Baba of Karo: A Woman of the Muslim Hausa*.[4] Accompanied by an introduction by M. G. Smith and extensive footnotes, *Baba* illustrates major themes in Hausa life and society--kinship and friendship, religion and economy, social norms and deviance.[5]

More recently, Marjorie Shostak has published *Nisa: The Life and Words of a !Kung Woman*, which explores the relationship between the !Kung and their changing ecological and political environment through the life of a single woman.[6] In the issue of violence *Nisa* raises questions about the typicalness of any given individual. Although the !Kung are known for their relatively pacific relations with one another, Shostak notes the unusual level of violence in Nisa's life. In addition to revealing much about Nisa and the !Kung, the book accomplishes what various theorists of the recording of life histories call for:[7] one learns important information about Shostak, her values, and her relationship with the !Kung and with Nisa as an individual. In the absence of this knowledge (we know virtually nothing of Mary Smith, for example) we are ill equipped to assess critically the presentation of the narrative.

A variety of disciplinary approaches and aims is found in Patricia W. Romero's *Life Histories of African Women*,[8] a collection of seven short life histories from six different societies and a broad range of time periods. Some are largely in the narrator's own words; others are biographical, relying upon historical documents. Still others mix both formats. The disciplinary approaches of the collectors of these narratives vary considerably. As life history and oral history develop further as fields of study, we can expect more models and further refinement of methodology.

The Narrative Texts

The three women included in this volume exemplify some of the class and ethnic diversity of Swahili society, although each is an individual with individual personality and tastes, not only a representative of a group. They were selected because they occupied different niches within Mombasa's social structure, reflected different world views within Swahili culture, and were interesting and approachable conversationalists as individuals. The interviews were conducted by Margaret Strobel in the women's homes in Swahili, without an interpreter. Ranging in age from mid-eighties to mid-fifties at the time of the interviews, the three reveal the preoccupations, options, stresses, and strategies of women who lived in a cosmopolitan Muslim city during the colonial and postcolonial periods in Kenya. Their lives illustrate a range of influence from European institutions and the variety of struggles that women face. All three life histories are in some ways "narratives of rebellion,"[9] even though not all three women would identify themselves as rebels. The oldest woman struggled for personal autonomy against the constraints of wifehood. The second enhanced the esteem of low-status descendants of slaves through *makungwi* associations, thereby challenging the social stratification of Swahili society. The third and youngest woman challenged more directly the sexist barriers in Swahili society by seeking Western education and pursuing a public political role.

Because these life histories are the result of a collaboration, the three women's lives as presented here also reflect the world view and interests of Margaret Strobel, who did the initial interviews in 1972-1973 and again in 1975, and Sarah Mirza, who participated in editorial decisions. And so, it is to this collaboration that we turn.

These interviews were part of Strobel's Ph.D. dissertation research. She had read *Baba of Karo*, which in the early 1970s was one of the very few pieces of scholarship about African women, and she had a vague notion of preparing some life histories--"Bibi of Mombasa" became the joking title of this half-formed project. (*Bibi* is a respectful Swahili term for a woman.) However, she conducted the initial interviews with each woman not to collect a life history but rather to discover the interests and historical activities of

Muslim women in Mombasa, about whom very little had been written. Strobel's interest in women's lives came from her own personal and intellectual commitment to feminism. Given the separation of the sexes in this Muslim society, her decision to focus on women as a separate group conformed to indigenous social categories. The disjuncture is great between her own personal values, which strongly advocate the equality of the sexes, racial or ethnic groups, and classes, and those of these women, who for the most part accept and envision a world, ordered by religion, in which sexes and classes are presumed to be unequal and ethnic groups often conflict. (The Islamic ideal does not sanction class and ethnic conflict, although it does admit a formal inequality, e.g., in divorce and inheritance rights, between men and women.) Although the interviews bear the imprint of Strobel's questions, she felt she was in Mombasa to learn about these people, not to convert them to her own viewpoint. Indeed, people rarely asked her opinion about things, and she rarely offered it. The affection that developed was based upon an implicit acceptance of each other's worlds and values.

As Strobel's relationship developed with each woman, the life history took on a direction dictated by the individual's own interests and activities.[10] Friends introduced Kaje wa Mwenye Matano (Bi Kaje) as an older woman who could speak generally about women's lives and activities. In the course of the discussions, a picture emerged of the household of slaves and freeborn people in which she grew up as the freeborn daughter of a poor but free Mombasa man and his slave concubine. Subsequent interviews covered life in Mombasa around the turn of the century.

The second woman, Mishi wa Abdala, emerged as a leader of one of Mombasa's groups of *makungwi*, women who conduct female life cycle rituals. In the course of attending numerous weddings, Strobel encountered the *makungwi*. Since they generally represented a different social stratum from that of the elites whom she had met to that point, she joined their dance group, paid her dues, and thereby gained access to the secret knowledge. Among those who knew the details of the rituals, Mishi wa Abdala (Ma Mishi) was the gentlest of the *makungwi*, who pride themselves on being frightening. Interviews with her consisted of clarifying the rituals that Strobel observed and confirming, with Ma Shea, another leader, the words for various wedding dances.

Strobel met the youngest woman, Shamsa Muhamad Muhashamy, known as Mwana Kutani, in the context of her leadership role in Swahili women's associations and in women's politics in Mombasa. Interviews with her were significantly different from those with the other two in the sense that she began at the beginning of her life and went chronologically through the events she felt were important. She described the history of one of these associations, the Muslim Women's Institute, and asked for a copy of the tape to keep as a historical record for the group itself.

Each woman no doubt had her own motivation for agreeing to the interviews. Although they are known among themselves and to outsiders as rather factious, the Swahili are also a generous and cosmopolitan people on the whole. (Indeed they may be no more factious than any other heterogeneous group.) The community of women had not encountered an inconsiderate scholar, hence there was no prior negative experience that would predispose them to refuse. Strobel did not think to ask why they agreed to give their life stories, but we can suggest some reasons. For Bi Kaje, approaching the end of her life and unable because of blindness to participate actively in daily life, the interviews may have functioned as a kind of review of her life, a summing up. [11]

For the *makungwi*, having the attention and participation in public wedding dances of a "European" was a distinct advantage in their competition with their rivals in Majengo, the newer part of Mombasa Island. Strobel agreed to honor the secret knowledge, which presumably strengthened her relationship with Ma Mishi. One anecdote may illustrate this. Although Strobel had met Mwana Kutani and Ma Mishi independently, they knew each other because the latter had worked for the former's brother as a cook. When asked by Mwana Kutani what the *makungwi* do in their puberty rites, Strobel replied that she could not reveal the secrets. This refusal was reported back to the *makungwi* and Ma Mishi, who retold the story with a certain pride. Ma Mishi may have been motivated by a desire to have the songs and rituals preserved for posterity, as she requested ten years later, even though she did not express this desire at the time.

As is clear from her narrative, Mwana Kutani has a strong sense of her historic role. She was interested in preserving the history of the various organizations she had helped found, and presumably saw this project as a way to accomplish that goal. It also served as an external validation of her work and life, which has at times been controversial.

Although the material from these interviews was used for Strobel's dissertaticn and for *Muslim Women in Mombasa, 1890-1975*,[12] the life histories themselves lay unprocessed until 1979, when she and Sarah Mirza began working together to check the transcriptions and edit the taped interviews. They had met in Nairobi at the initial stages of Strobel's research but had no inkling of a future collaboration.

Sarah Mirza was born in Mombasa and is a native speaker of Kimvita, Mombasa's dialect of Swahili. Having a B.A. in Linguistics from the University of Nairobi, she has taught Swahili at the University of Wisconsin--Madison, at UCLA, and independently. She coauthored *Kiswahili: A Foundation for Speaking, Reading, and Writing*.[13]

We prepared the manuscript cooperatively during several work sessions spread out over a period of ten years and individually in between. Some of the tapes had been transcribed in Mombasa by various paid and volunteer workers. These were checked and the rest were transcribed by Mirza and Strobel working together. Although both contributed to each part of the process, the translations were largely the responsibility of Sarah Mirza and the editing that of Margaret Strobel. Similarly Strobel prepared the English notes and sociohistorical portion of the English introduction; Mirza, the Swahili notes, the Swahili introduction, and the sociolinguistic portion of the English introduction. Strobel prepared the manuscript for publication.

Finally, in December 1983 Sarah Mirza took the first draft to Mombasa to gain the three women's approval, once again, for the project. Each had consented over ten years earlier to have her life history published, but ethics and practical considerations indicated that the material should be checked and confirmed and permission received again. In the case of Bi Kaje, now deceased, her companion, Zuena Ali, was pleased that people would come to know about Bi Kaje. Ma Mishi, who subsequently died, also enthusiastically agreed to publication. Characteristically, Shamsa Muhamad Muhashamy energetically confirmed the contents of her interview. Arrangements were made to share any royalties that might result from publication.

Mombasa as a Swahili City

Located near the equator, Mombasa has existed as a maritime community since at least the eleventh century.[14] Over the centuries immigrants came by land and sea, populating Mombasa Island and the surrounding mainland with racially and ethnically diverse peoples. Coming from the north, the ancestors of the present-day Twelve Tribes formed the core of what might be called the indigenous population, which ancestry Bi Kaje claims. The Twelve Tribes came to be organized into two confederations, the Three Tribes (Kilindini, Changamwe, and Tangana) and the Nine Tribes (Mvita, Kilifi, Mtwapa, Jomvu, Pate, Faza, Shaka, Bajun, and Katwa or Somali).

Mombasa existed as an independent city-state alongside other Swahili towns through the dynasties of Mwana Mkisi (a woman) and Sheik Mvita, who replaced her ca. 1300 and who was associated with the Nine Tribes. The Portuguese controlled Mombasa from 1593 to 1698, during which time the earlier migration continued: Twelve Tribes people, Indian traders, some Hadrami from the southern portion of Arabia, some Omani Arabs from the Persian Gulf area. During the seventeenth century because of the rivalry between the Three Tribes and the Nine Tribes, the Yarubi dynasty ruled from Oman, increasing the migration of soldiers and administrators from that area. During this period some of Mwana Kutani's ancestors arrived in Mombasa. In 1730 the Yarubi appointed the Mazrui clan to govern Mombasa, which they did until 1837, mediating between the now well established confederations of the Nine Tribes and Three Tribes. When the Busaidi dynasty overthrew the Yarubi in Oman, the Mazrui in Mombasa were unable for several reasons to continue their role as mediators. With the assistance of the Kilindini, one of the Three Tribes, the Busaidi invaded Mombasa and added it to their growing sphere of influence in the Indian Ocean.

Prior to the Busaidi period, the Twelve Tribes had established close ties to the Mijikenda peoples on the immediate hinterland, a relationship identified in Swahili as *utani*.[15] The Mijikenda were themselves a collection of nine groups (the Digo and Duruma, allied with the Three Tribes; the Giriama, Kauma, Kambe, Ribe, Chonyi, Jibana, and Rabai, allied with various of the Nine Tribes). Derogatorily

called the "Nyika" (bush), some Mijikenda converted to Islam
and merged with the Swahili on the coast. Others were
enslaved or pawned and similarly joined the Swahili
community, albeit as subordinates and dependents. As the
Busaidi period progressed, the ties between the Mijikenda and
the Twelve Tribes came to be based more on individual
economic interactions and less on corporate links. Swahili
traders moved into Mijikenda territory and bought the latter's
surplus grain; Swahili caravans used Mijikenda porters to
carry ivory to the coast.

Thus over the centuries, alliances did not follow racial or
even ethnic lines. Rather, pursuing their own interests in a
fluid fashion, factions of Swahilis or Arabs or Mijikenda allied
and split. With intermarriage and concubinage, the racial
composition of the coastal population became mixed, so that
ethnic identification, racial characteristics, and social status
were not completely congruent.

During the period of Busaidi rule from 1837 to 1895, the
slave trade expanded significantly, especially following the
movement of the Busaidi capital from Masqat in the Persian
Gulf to Zanzibar off the Tanzanian coast in 1840. Mombasa
was a slave-importing community, which brought another
significant migration from the slave-yielding areas of east and
central Africa, notably present-day Tanzania, Mozambique,
and Malawi.[16] In this way Ma Mishi's ancestors came to
Mombasa.

The expansion of the Swahili onto the mainland
accompanied the establishment of farms using slave labor. In
contrast to Malindi to the north, where a plantation slave
system developed, slavery in Mombasa remained a more
face-to-face relationship between owner and slave. Many
slaves worked for wages, the owner receiving half. Men got
jobs as artisans, laborers, or sailors; women, as cooks or
nannies.

As the Busaidi sultans in Zanzibar grew increasingly
dependent upon British support, they were forced in stages to
restrict first the slave trade and then slavery itself. In 1888
the administration of the ten-mile strip of the coast that
represented the sultan's domains, called *mwambao*, was
turned over to the Imperial British East Africa Company as a
concession in exchange for 11,000 pounds rent. In 1895 that
part of the domain in present-day Kenya became the East
African Protectorate, later joined with Kenya Colony, under

British rule. (Tanganyika was by then a German territory, which led to significant battles being fought in east Africa during World War One.)

Colonialism changed the relationship of the coast to the hinterland. Instead of being a relatively small area linked to the coast by religious, familial, or corporate ties, the hinterland expanded and became connected to the coast more clearly and exclusively through money and power.

As part of a British colony, Mombasa experienced tremendous expansion, becoming the largest seaport in east Africa. It grew from a Muslim community with a population of about 25,000 at the turn of the century to a cosmopolitan city of 100,000 by about 1950, and over 340,000 by the time of the 1979 census. The migration of Africans from upcountry transformed the culturally Muslim community into an even more diverse city, in which Muslims by the 1960s were the minority. Old Town, the area of original settlement, remains a Muslim Swahili community. But the newer settlements on the island and those spread onto the surrounding mainland were more eclectic.

British colonialism altered the earlier patterns of alliance and identification. The more fluid (albeit unequal) precolonial relationships (clientage, slavery, political alliances) over time crystalized around ethnic and regional identification, although even these identifications fluctuated according to changing political contexts. The colonial administration used the Arab administrative infrastructure to govern the coast and shared with Arabs a sense of the cultural superiority of Arab culture. Thus in the racial hierarchy of civilization as defined by the colonizers, Europeans ranked on top; Indians, second; Arabs, third; and Africans, on the bottom. This angered Twelve Tribes people, with their tradition of long residence, Muslim culture, and Swahili civilization. But it also led some Arab-Swahili people to identify as Arabs, just as the triumph of African nationalism has led some Arab-Swahili people to identify now as African.

The three women whose lives are recorded here represent portions of the Swahili community. All were born just before or within the first quarter-century of British administration. Bi Kaje is the daughter of a Three Tribes man and his Mijikenda concubine. At the time of the interviews she lived in Changamwe on the mainland northwest of Mombasa Island. Ma Mishi's grandparents

were Makua slaves brought from Mozambique. She lives in
Kaloleni, a multiethnic community on the island that was
settled in the 1920s and 1930s primarily by upcountry
migrants, although other Swahili and Arab families live
there as well. Of Omani and Hadrami Arab ancestry,
Mwana Kutani lives in a neighborhood of Old Town called
Mjua Kale. Although these three women represent a
sampling of the various groups that make up the Swahili
community in Mombasa, there are ethnic groups missing.
Baluchi soldiers were brought by the Zanzibari sultan. Their
descendants have intermarried with local Swahili and speak
Kimvita, the Mombasa dialect. More recent Hadrami
migrants called Shihiri form a part of the community,
although they retain more elements of Hadrami culture and
Arabic language than do the descendants of earlier Hadrami
migrants.

   In many ways these three typify the experience of
Swahili women. They all married more than once. Typically,
parents arranged the first marriage; subsequent unions were
more likely to be initiated by the couple themselves. By
Muslim law as articulated on the coast, a father or
grandfather may marry a virgin daughter off without her
permission; a previously married nonvirgin must give her
consent. However, the father or grandfather is encouraged to
obtain the girl's permission, even in the former case. Any
other category of guardian cannot marry the girl off without
her permission.[17]

   After marriage it was not uncommon for the couple to
live with the wife's parents or in housing owned by her.
Bishop Steere noted in 1870 that on the "Swahili coast . . .
the bride's father or family should find her a house and that
the husband should go to live with her, not she with him."[18]
In Lamu, freeborn families provided an elaborate house for
their daughter as a bride in order to cement ties with
outsiders through marriage, without risking their daughters
being taken away with the foreign husband.[19] Living in her
own home gave Bi Kaje substantial security and leverage in
her unsuccessful marriages.

   First marriages frequently ended in divorce, contributing
to an overall high divorce rate. Statistics from 1915 to 1950
from Muslim communities in Kenya indicate a consistent
pattern of one divorce for every two marriages.[20] Under the
school of law practiced on the coast, a man need give no

reason for divorcing his wife. A woman can gain a divorce in case of impotence, serious disease of the husband, or nonmaintenance. Bi Kaje was granted a divorce from her first husband, Muhamadi, on the latter grounds. Alternatively, she might offer her husband money to divorce her, or relinquish claim to any unpaid portion of her bridal gift. Failing all else, she could make his life miserable until he divorced her himself.[21] This was Bi Kaje's approach to her second husband. Of the three, only Ma Mishi reported a long-lasting affectionate marital relationship--with her second husband.[22]

Both religion and custom reinforce the norms of male authority in the marital relationship. Contemporary Mombasa Swahili residents, male and female, affirm the right of a husband to make crucial decisions regarding the family and attribute this authority to Islam. Women's power, according to Marc J. Swarz, comes from men's emotional need to maintain their marital intimacy in the absence of other sources of intimacy. Women, on the other hand, have rich intimate and emotional relationships with other women and with their children and are thus less dependent emotionally on men.[23] In addition to Islam, Ma Mishi's account of puberty rituals illustrates customary, non-Islamic reinforcement of male dominance.

Infertility has been common on the coast.[24] Mwana Kutani had no children; Ma Mishi had only one. Bi Kaje was fortunate to have five children, although only one survived into adulthood. Because the relationship between mother and child is a close and important one, women--all three in this instance--often fostered children if they themselves had few or none.

All three women lived in households composed mostly of women, a pattern that is not the predominant residence pattern, but is not uncommon. The 1969 census showed 10,703 female heads of household, out of a total of 66,815 heads of household (16.5%). These 10,703 female heads of household compare with 29,265 wives of heads of household. Thus the number of female heads of household is more than one-third the number of wives of male heads of household.[25] These figures include the whole of Mombasa, not only the Swahili community. However, an older survey of only Old Town suggests a similar pattern.[26] Collected in the late 1940s by Leo Silberman, the data from the study suggest

that 13% of Old Town households were headed by women.
Household heads ("chief breadwinners") were categorized by
occupation. If one takes the 69 heads identified as
"supported" (3.7% of breadwinners), and the 108 heads who
are prostitutes (5.8%), and adds to them an estimated 70
women who refused to give information (84 respondents,
"mainly women," refused to answer questions), the total is
247 female heads of household out of 1,943, or 12.7%.
Although all three women lived in female households, only Bi
Kaje and Ma Mishi had to support themselves, working in
typically female occupations.

Even if they represent a minority in terms of residence
pattern, the female-oriented experience of these women is
typical of Muslim women in Mombasa. Because of the
separation of the sexes, men and women mix very rarely on
social occasions.[27] In homes today there is still relatively
little time spent in sexually mixed groups. In offices men and
women work together and socialize, which offers an
opportunity for young people to meet and select their own
mates (and which explains the past opposition of Muslim
elders to the education of girls for employment).

The life histories give evidence of the rich festive,
ceremonial, and ritual experiences of women. Ma Mishi and
Shamsa Muhashamy are more involved in women's organized
activities than was Bi Kaje. As an adult Bi Kaje participated
briefly in the early version of lelemama, the dance form that
occupied many of Mwana Kutani's years as a young married
woman. But Bi Kaje's lelemama is a much more staid and
traditional dance. Women's lelemama groups complemented
men's groups, which were called beni, bwaride, or gwaride.[28]
Carefully separating the women and men, the dance groups
provided a major form of creative cultural expression and
celebration. They also reproduced the tendency to factions
found often in Swahili communities.[29] The original groups,
Kingi (from "King") and Kilungu, gave way to new groups,
although the former contained the core of the Old Town elites
and their slaves or dependents. Kingi was noted for its
Omani Arab and Nine Tribes members and their dependents.
Kilungu had a more ethnically diverse membership,
apparently less affluent overall, including a core of Three
Tribes members like Bi Kaje herself. The groups with which
Mwana Kutani and Ma Mishi were associated, Banu Saada,
Ibinaal Watan, and Combine, developed titles for officers that

reflected the changing political milieu. The Arab and Swahili officers *sheha* (sheik), *waziri* (ministers), and *wazee* (elders) of Kingi and Kilungu gave way to *kwini* (queen), *maduki* (dukes), *maledi* (ladies), *daktari* (doctor), and others. Mwana Kutani transfered the skills developed in *lelemama* associations to the Muslim Women's Institute, a more Western-style social and welfare association. Ma Mishi spent much of her life as a leader of *makungwi*, women who conduct life cycle rituals.

Bi Kaje's discussion of the rituals of the *makungwi* (s. *kungwi)* varies considerably from that of Ma Mishi. The former's disdain toward the activities of the *makungwi* and the culture of slaves typifies freeborn people's attitude. The *makungwi* themselves feed the reputation of toughness and cruelty, but with a different aim, character development, as Ma Mishi notes in her story. Bi Kaje asserts that most slaves, particularly those in towns, acculturated to freeborn ways and dropped these rituals. Whatever the numerical truth, the rituals continued and formed a female and slave/ex-slave subculture in Mombasa. However, none of the three has been a participant in *pepo* spirit possession cults that many coastal women join.[30]

These three women present a picture of colonialism as a relatively benign institution. Mwana Kutani, in her family's quest for her education, encountered colonial discrimination and sexism. All felt the impact of colonialism in its resulting demographic and cultural changes: the enormous immigration of upcountry people, for example. But in their complaints, they do not identify colonialism as the culprit. Overall, none speaks with great bitterness toward the British. To the extent that the coastal Swahili benefited from the view that Arabic civilization and Islam were superior, they did not see the British as exploitative colonizers. In addition, their attitude is in part a result of the nationalist experience in Kenya, which involved upcountry peoples more than coastal groups. Indigenous Mombasa people did not experience the direct dislocations from the land that many upcountry peoples did, nor were they forced into laboring on white settler farms. Finally, with the cultural and political ascendance of upcountry peoples following the achieving of independence in 1963, many coastal Swahili people feel themselves a cultural, religious, and political minority. As such, one finds at times a sense of the colonial period as "the good old days," not out of

their love for the British but rather nostalgia for a period of
greater Swahili cultural autonomy.
    These texts give little feel for the city of Mombasa as a
whole today. Even Mwana Kutani, who is most involved in
politics and larger social affairs, speaks little of non-Swahili
women. Their silences on many of the dislocations of the
colonial and postcolonial period speak to the insularity of
Swahili women's lives. As traditonal women, Bi Kaje and Ma
Mishi had little or no direct experience with political
movements. Both had lived outside Old Town, in ethnically
diverse neighborhoods, but their reflections do not suggest
close ties to non-Swahili people. In excerpts not included in
these texts, Bi Kaje comments upon the dances performed by
Nyamwezi and other people, and her comments evidence a
familiarity with various languages and customs (often via the
slaves in her household). But her world is basically a Swahili
world. It is, of course, risky to draw firm conclusions about
what people do *not* say. Had Strobel asked more directly
about relations with non-Swahili people. a different picture
might have been drawn. But, Strobel's experience affirms
the silences: in a year of visiting at weddings, mealtime, and
teatime, she encountered very few non-Swahili guests in the
homes of these three women and her other friends.
    These texts are products of a particular time and place:
Mombasa in the early and middle 1970s. Not only do they
represent Kimvita, they were collected in a period of
relatively greater prosperity and, consequently, leisure.
Inflation has forced changes. Women perform the wedding
dances--both *lelemama* and the *makungwi*'s dances--less
frequently because of reduced expenditures made on
weddings. Moreover, in subsequent visits to Mombasa, Sarah
Mirza found that people have less time and inclination to talk.
In some cases the women are working longer and harder to
make ends meet. In others, they have less interest in things
past. Shamsa Muhashamy observed this herself, though she
was speaking about the mid-1970s: "These days, because of
the way life is, everyone is hectic, a person can't take time
for someone else." We are grateful that she, Bi Kaje. and Ma
Mishi took the time to share their lives with us.

PART I

Kaje wa Mwenye Matano

Shamsa Muhamad Muhashamy and family, 1973
Photograph by Margaret Strobel

Shamsa Muhamad Muhashamy, 1973
Photograph by Margaret Strobel

Introduction

Bi Kaje, the oldest of the three women, was born around 1890. When the Uganda Railroad was first being built in Mombasa in 1896, she had not yet reached puberty but was old enough to understand what was going on. She married her first husband just before slavery was abolished in 1907. Thus at the time of our discussions, she was in her early eighties. We talked in Old Town and at her home in Changamwe where she lived with her companion, Ma Zuena, in a typical single story Swahili house with a thatched roof. She was slightly built, with large holes stretched in her earlobes from jewelry no longer inserted. She wore two cloths, *leso*, draped according to traditional fashion. Although blind and somewhat hard of hearing, she was alert and appeared to have a good memory. Our conversations were a combination of things about which she wished to reminisce and those in which Strobel was particularly interested. She made few concessions to Strobel's unfamiliarity with Kimvita, Mombasa's dialect of Swahili, using old words and Kimvita tense markers. Perhaps her blindness, combined with her age, contributed to her shaping the discussions in the directions she wished: not being distracted by seeing her interviewer, she might more easily lapse into self-oriented reminiscence. More than Ma Mishi or Mwana Kutani, Bi Kaje introduced topics that she found interesting and spoke in detail about events that had moved her. At first, she may have found our conversations an interesting diversion, since she was unable to contribute to the domestic work of the household or do many other things. As we continued to meet, she seemed to view them with more seriousness. One day

Strobel arrived while she was visiting with some other older
women from the neighborhood. After a short time, she stood
up and said to me, "Let's go, we have work to do." Her age
and infirmity also made lengthier interviews possible. since
she was not troubled by other business or chores. Thus the
greater length of her section is explained by a combination of
her leisure and loquaciousness.

As her story reveals, Bi Kaje does not question most of
the old values. Instead, for the most part she accepts and
explains them without defensiveness, even when she is
criticizing the lack of religious education given to girls and the
vulnerability of orphan children. She came into close contact
with people who followed new ways, notably the children and
grandchildren of her companion, Ma Zuena. She matter-of-
factly identifies forces of change, for example, girls' secular
education. Even where she disapproves of change, she does
not attack others or express bitterness.

Her world and values also reflect those of a freeborn
Twelve Tribes person. Despite the passing of decades since
the abolition of slavery, her consciousness of cultural
superiority that comes from being a Muslim and a freeborn
descendant of the Twelve Tribes emerges in various chapters.

Bi Kaje died in 1981 or 1982. Surviving members of
her close family did not attend her funeral. She did not have
particularly good relations with close relatives while she was
alive, which was part of her reason for living with Ma Zuena,
with whom she became close friends later in life.

Family

Bi Kaje's account of her family reveals interesting
features of Swahili kinship. She uses classificatory kinship
terms; thus one of her "grandmothers," Bi Hindi, who headed
the household of slave and freeborn people, is a distant
relative of Bi Kaje's father's mother's mother, Binti Kombo.
Bi Hindi becomes important to her because her father,
Mwenye Matano, lives and works as a dependent of Bi Hindi.
Similarly, she does not differentiate between cousins and
siblings, daughters and nieces, which makes her account
occasionally confusing and ambiguous in English.

Despite the strong patrilineal bias of Islam, one's
maternal kin are vitally important. Indeed, although the

child of a freeborn man is legally free, having a freeborn mother is an important sign of high social status. A person with free descent on both sides is a *mwungwana* (pl. *waungwana*).[1] Since Arabs as outsiders established themselves on the coast by marrying into Twelve Tribes families by the process Bi Kaje notes, Twelve Tribes women played an important role as intermediaries. Pat Caplan notes that in parts of the Swahili coast, descent is reckoned cognatically, through both males and females, even more than is the case in Mombasa.[2] She links this cognatic descent to a subsistence mode of production, communal land holding, and an emphasis on custom *(mila)*, in contrast to patriliny, greater integration into a capitalist mode of production, individual landownership, and Islamic law *(sheria)*.

Bi Kaje's views on the status hierarchy in Mombasa distinctly represent those of a Twelve Tribes person. She places the indigenous Twelve Tribes at the core of Mombasa. She identifies the Arabs, including Omani Arabs, as outsiders who were not automatically accorded respect. This attitude corrects a view commonly held in the literature of the coast, which was written during the colonial period and inherited the colonialists' view of the Omani aristocrats as superior to Africans. This Arab ascendance in the historiography reflected the rise of the Omani sultanate in Zanzibar in the nineteenth century, but has been misread backwards into earlier periods.[3]

In our interviews, her mention of historical incidents contributed little to what is already known; indeed, it contained inaccuracies. This pattern reflects the relative ignorance of most women of such matters of the public domain as the political history of the area.[4]

Slavery

Raised as a freeborn woman within a household of slaves, freed slaves, *wazalia* (people of slave descent born in the household), and freeborn folk, Bi Kaje holds the views and values of freeborn culture. She characterizes as cruel and stupid the female puberty rites that some slaves continued to practice. To the extent that slaves acculturated to freeborn Swahili norms and practices and converted to Islam, they became acceptable to Bi Kaje and other freeborn members of

the community. They were no longer *washenzi*, or
barbarians. But status distinctions remained. They had to
act deferentially toward freeborn people, not wearing shoes in
their owners' presence, for example. Slaves were not
commonly given the names of the Prophet and His
descendants. Thus there emerges a mixed picture of slavery
and slaves through Bi Kaje's eyes. On the one hand, she
attributes the pawning or enslavement of Mijikenda to their
own stupidity rather than to economic hardship or famine.
On the other, she records respect and affection for many of
the slaves she knew.

     As is common in other accounts of slavery, house slaves
in Mombasa had closer relations with their owners and
perhaps an easier life than farm slaves. Conditions for slaves
generally were easier in places like Mombasa than in the
plantation economies of Zanzibar or Malindi to the north,
where the integration into an international capitalist economy
led to maximizing production.[5] Bi Kaje held that slavery in
Bi Hindi's household was not very harsh. It is difficult to
confirm this claim, to separate out a romanticization of
slavery on her part. It is important to note that Bi Kaje is
speaking about the very end of the slave period. At her birth,
the British were already forcing the Sultan of Zanzibar to
restrict the trading and ownership of slaves. In 1907, just
after her marriage, the British abolished slavery. In the
period between, the establishment of colonial rule, the
development of Mombasa as a port, and the construction of
the Uganda Railroad brought enormous economic changes,
which gave freed slaves opportunities for autonomy that
would not have been possible in 1850. Bi Kaje notes that
after abolition some slaves left (for example, Hidaya), or no
longer brought to their former owner her share of the
earnings. However, others chose to continue the pattern of
social relations dictated by slavery, presumably drawn by the
fact of their acculturation and the security of their continued
dependence upon their former owners. These people came to
celebrations, as in the case of Hatimjawe, or continued out of
"friendship" to do the household chores. Not surprisingly,
these freed slaves who chose to maintain a dependent
relationship are the ones whom Bi Kaje recalls best.

     Her reconstruction of slavery combines 1970s contexts
with early twentieth-century values. In asking about
slavery, Strobel asked for factual information about

individual slaves whom Bi Kaje had mentioned, not about how people felt about being or owning slaves. Bi Kaje's comments on slavery were largely self-initiated and self-selected. However, ever though the occasional questions put to her were neutral on the question of slavery, Bi Kaje adopted a defensive posture in insisting upon the non-exploitativeness of slavery in Bi Hindi's household. Despite her relative imperviousness to other political or cultural influences, she is affected by the changed political context in independent Kenya, in which the past ownership of some Africans by other Africans and Afro-Arabs is criticized. But her description of the financial transactions between owners and slaves who work elsewhere for wages (for example Saada and Mtenzi) reflects a highly personalized, not yet fully commoditized, relationship.

Although some slaves joined the social networks of their owners as dependents, not all lost ties with their own kin. Those taken from east-central Africa had these ties severed. But locally enslaved people from among the Mijikenda might be redeemed, as was Majaliwa by his father. Of the thirty slaves from Bi Hindi's household about whom there is solid information (see Table 1), nearly half came from east-central Africa (Tanzania, Mozambique, or Malawi). More than one-

TABLE 1
ORIGINS OF SLAVES IN BI HINDI'S HOUSEHOLD

East-central Africa	14
Mijikenda	12
Other Kenya	1
Mixed	1
Unknown	2
Total	30

third were Mijikenda.[6]

Situated in an urban community, many Mombasa slaves performed domestic work within the household and worked for wages in urban jobs, bringing half of their wages to their owner. Table 2 represents the occupations of the slaves mentioned by Bi Kaje. Notably, only 20% of the slaves whose occupations were known worked on Bi Hindi's or her dependents' farms. Moreover, female and male slaves in comparable numbers worked for wages, although six women and no men worked as domestic slaves within the household

TABLE 2
SLAVE OCCUPATIONS

Occupation	Female	Male
Farm labor	3	3
Within household		
Nanny	1	0
Cook	1	0
Food buyer	1	0
Concubine	2	0
Miscellaneous	1	0
Subtotal	6	0
Wage labor or self-employed		
Porter, carrier	0	2
Boat conductor	0	2
Food seller	0	1
Cook	5	0
Carpenter	0	1
Casual laborer, own business	2	2
Subtotal	7	8
Unknown	3	0
TOTAL	19	11

itself. This domestic labor underscores the point made by Claire C. Robertson and Martin A. Klein that free women in Africa were major beneficiaries of slavery, since a significant portion of slave labor was work assigned to women.[7] Commonly female slaves were hired by Indian families, who were forbidden by British law to own slaves. Although both female and male slaves worked for wages, the variety of male occupations greatly exceeded that of female. Marcia Wright notes the consequences of this: following abolition women continued to have fewer options to pursue.[8]

From Bi Kaje's account we can construct some sense of the family life of the slaves in this household (see Table 3). The first impression is that remarkably high numbers of slaves neither married nor were concubines (7 women and 4 men), and many had no children (4 married women, 1 married man, and, as far as we know, none of the 11 unmarried people). It is unclear why these slaves did not marry, given the importance of marriage as a norm in both

TABLE 3
SLAVE MARRIAGE AND FERTILITY*

Marital Status	Had no children	Had children	Total # of children
Females married	4	5	7***
Concubines	0	2	5
Males married**	1	4	7***
Females not married or concubines	7	0	0
Males not married**	4	0	0

*Females: n=18 adults (1 female died as a grown child).
Males: n=9 adults (1 male died young, 1 male's marital and
fertility status is unknown).
**Assumed not to have children if none were mentioned.
***Includes one child of free status in each category. Due to
overlap from slaves being married to each other, there are a
total of eleven individual children born to slaves married to
other slaves or to free men. These eleven, combined with five
children born to concubines, total sixteen births.

Swahili society and the areas from which they came.
Possibly, some of these people married after abolition, when
Bi Kaje was less likely to be in touch with them. Whatever
the explanation, the vulnerability of the women in particular
as they grew older with no children to support them doubtless
increased their dependence upon their former owners.

Slave marriage was regulated by Islamic law and
supervised by the slave's owner, who had to give permission.
(This became the crux of legal battles between ex-slave
owners and former slaves following abolition until the 1920s.
The former claimed that only an owner could free a slave, not
the British government, hence their right to control marriage
was intact.)[9] A female slave could be married to someone
else, slave or free, without being first freed. The children of
two slaves belonged to the mother's owner.

Slave fertility was low in Mombasa. Only a total of
sixteen births are found in Bi Hindi's household among slaves
married to each other or by concubines (totaling eleven adult
parents). Of these sixteen, only two-thirds, or eleven,
survived to adulthood. Such low fertility was not unique to
Mombasa. Scholars have found a similar pattern in Lamu
and elsewhere on the coast.[10] Disease, high infant mortality,
breastfeeding of children, and recourse to abortion explain the
low fertility. Claude Meillassoux speculates that slave
fertility was low generally throughout Africa.[11] Other

Mombasa. Scholars have found a similar pattern in Lamu
and elsewhere on the coast.[10] Disease, high infant mortality,
breastfeeding of children, and recourse to abortion explain the
low fertility. Claude Meillassoux speculates that slave
fertility was low generally throughout Africa.[11] Other
sources for the Swahili coast indicate that freeborn people
had low fertility too,[12] as was the case for Bi Hindi herself,
and for Ma Mishi and Mwana Kutani in this volume.

Abolition came in 1907 at the hands of the colonial
government, which compensated slave owners. Prior to
abolition, some slaves, pawns like Majaliwa, were ransomed
by relatives; others were freed as a religious act. As was the
case elsewhere on the coast,[13] the legal change did not reflect
a change in the realities of everyone's life. Some chose the
security that dependency offered; others opted for the new
economic opportunities that accompanied colonial expansion
in the early part of the century. Bi Kaje makes it clear that
some ex-slaves refused to continue the old practices, although
elsewhere she suggests that ex-owners no longer demanded
their customary half of a slave's wages.

Seclusion and Veiling

Bi Kaje was raised in more strict seclusion than either
Mwana Kutani or Ma Mishi, a function of both her greater
age and the high social position but traditional views of her
family. As we will discover, the limitation of the freeborn
woman's mobility could make her life complicated in times of
crisis. But Bi Kaje did not experience seclusion as unduly
restrictive. She notes, also, its variability. Older women,
widows for whom remarriage was not an issue, would travel
in public and run errands for younger female family
members. Slave women, of course, did not observe purdah;
they carried the cloth that shielded freeborn women. After
abolition veiling appears to have increased. Lower-class
women observed increasingly high standards of seclusion as a
means of asserting higher social status.[14]

Kinship Diagram for
Kaje wa Mwenye Matano

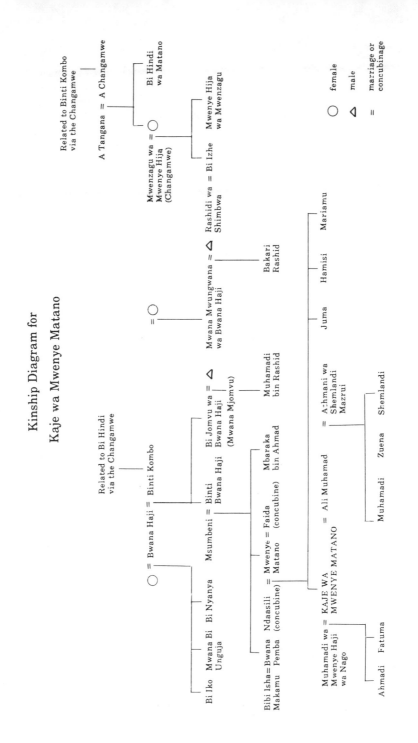

My Family

My father was born here in Mombasa, and my mother too. Both were natives of Mombasa. My father's parent, and my father's grandfather's parent, and my father's mother's parent all came from here. My father was named Mwenye Matano. His father was named Msumbeni. He came from Pemba, and married my grandmother, who gave birth to my father, Mwenye Matano bin Msumbeni.

My mother was named Ndaasili.[1] She died from fever when I was about seven years old. She bore four children. I am the eldest. The second is named Jumaa. She bore a third named Hamisi, and a fourth named Mariamu. The two youngest died while small; Jumaa died as an adult. He had married and had a child; first he died, then his child died.

I was born on Mombasa Island. If someone wanted to stay on their farm, fine, they stayed. But we were all born on Mombasa Island. I was born there near the Shikeli Mosque. Then we left there and came to live in Kibokoni. In Kibokoni there is a mosque, the Mahuru [freed slave] Mosque, near the Baluchis' houses. My father and mother lived there with my grandmother Bi Hindi until I was born. We four siblings were all born right there. Then when my grandmother died, we were taken by her younger sister, Bi Nyanya, Binti Bwana Haji's sister. The one who raised me was named Mwana Mjomvu. Her younger sister did too. It was she who took us, and we went to Kibokoni. After we had moved, the buildings were destroyed, and the whole place was torn down. Now they have all died.

It was she [Bi Nyanya] who took me there and raised me. My mother didn't raise the children. When she had given birth, that was it, my father's mother took the child; we were raised by our grandmother. My younger sibling was raised by a slave, Baadadhiki. Another person named Mefundi, also a slave, raised the next-younger sibling. Only the third-youngest was raised by my mother, then she died very young. My father had already died when my mother raised her.

Mwenye Matano's Work

My father oversaw his mother's [Bi Hindi's][2] farm. Then his mother told him, "Farm life doesn't suit you. Go to work at Kurwitu there at Shimo la Tewa." He took clothing and sold it to the people there. Some of them were fools. He brought pieces of cloth[3] and sold them. Those people had no money; they bartered with lots of varieties of food. My father called helpers. They came and got the food and took it from town to town to Indians' stores. It was sold, and the money was taken to Bi Hindi. His own work was to sew caps, these white caps that are a mark of being Swahili. While sitting there waiting for his sales to be completed, he sewed. If he sewed one cap it was thirty-two shillings (in shillings, back then it was sixteen rupees). And men's kaftans--if a person brought his own cloth, father would sew a decorated kaftan. He earned sixteen shillings; back then it was eight rupees. That was his only work, and the money flowed in. In the old days many foods were cheap. Servants farmed and brought coconuts, mangoes, all kinds of fruits to the house. So you didn't need to buy food. Cash from the sale of caps was put aside; the money from everything he did was set aside.

Bi Hindi

Bi Hindi was an important person in Mombasa, not because she was rich, but because of her birth.[4] We do not measure importance by wealth; we measure it by birth. If a rich person hasn't good ancestry, it is worth nothing among us. Only rich? So what. Bi Hindi had only two farms. Her husbands bought these for her. Both her first and second husbands bought her slaves and gave her farms. At the time of her divorce, he didn't take them away from her. He went on his way. I didn't have the opportunity to know her first husband, but the second was named Mwinyi Kitoja.

Binti Bwana Haji bore my father. Her sister was
named Bi Jomvu [Mwana Mjomvu] wa Bwana Haji. My
father's grandmother who gave birth to Mwana Mjomvu and
Binti Bwana Haji was Binti Kombo. Binti Kombo didn't have
anything. In the old days people didn't have anything. She
had farms, but what were they worth back then? You could
buy a farm for fifty shillings. And if they felt a farm wasn't
worth anything, and a person was having a hard time with it,
they sold it. Bi Hindi and Binti Kombo were related through
the Changamwe. Between the two of them, Bi Hindi didn't
have a child.

The Swahili

The Swahili are the kernel of Mombasa, indeed the
navel of this town. Now, if a European converts, they
become an Arab by tribe. That is, a European does not have
an African tribe, so if they convert, they become an Arab,
because they don't have Swahili blood.[5]
I am a Changamwe.[6] My tribe on my father's side is
Shirazi. I am Changamwe because my grandmother Bi Hindi
is Tangana; my grandmother Binti Kombo is Changamwe;
my father is entirely a person from here. But my father's
father is Shirazi.[7]
We Twelve Tribes alone are from the heart of Mombasa.
The Comorian among us is a stranger.[8] The European is a
foreigner; the Indian is a stranger; the Arab is a foreigner.
This is not their place. When the Arab came in the past and
wanted a wife, he couldn't marry someone's daughter from
here. If he came, he would be told, "Who is this person?"
We didn't want intermarriage with those Arabs. Perhaps he
was a slave back home. He wasn't allowed to marry
anybody's daughter. Then Ma Zuena's paternal grandfather
came, and he's the one who began the practice of
intermarriage. That is, Zuena's paternal grandmother is a
Changamwe. Her grandfather is an Arab, Hinawiy. Zuena's
grandfather on his mother's side is a *sharifu*.[9] And those
masharifu mix with people from here. We accept them. We
can't refuse the *masharifu*.
In the old days we couldn't understand everything; that
is, our elders told us some things and withheld others. They
held back--they said, "When young people are still young,
they are not told everything." They told half the story and

guarded the rest. Do you know what the origin of this censoring is? For instance, you have a brother who marries someone's slave, she will bear a child and that slave's owners are still around. Now if you are told about this, as a youngster you might quarrel and say, "Your mother is a slave of so-and-so." So, the elders watched their words. They feared the children would squabble, they would begin to throw dirty words at one another.

In other cases, a person converts to Islam, for example, a Mijikenda. A person says, "I want to become a Muslim," along with his wife. He will convert, he will become a Muslim, he will be taken to the mosque, he prays, he fasts during Ramadhan. Now, if he has a child, that child isn't anyone's slave. The father isn't a slave, he has converted. Or, a European comes and wants to join our religion. I ask you, whose slave is he? The thing that he has changed is his religion, that's all. He has refused his own religion and wants another. He is no one's slave. He left his place, he has come himself, "I want your religion, that of the Swahili people." So if he converts, he is not anyone's slave. A person who leaves his religion and follows ours has surpassed us. In praying, in fasting, he has surpassed those of us who were born into the hand of Islam. But for us, if a person leaves Islam and follows another religion, then he or she offends God very much. He does not like it at all.

Slavery

Bi Hindi's Gifts

My father had slaves; he didn't buy them himself. He had farms given to him by Bi Hindi, who raised him. She divided one farm and gave my father half. She gave him two slaves: one was named Faida, one Takosani. She divided the farm again and gave the remaining half to my uncle. She gave my uncle Mbaraka bin Ahmadi the farm and two slaves, Hidaya and Mtenzi.

We were young when our father died. But even when we had grown, we were only given a pittance. Our uncles, our father's brothers, used it for themselves. They ate it up, so that when the children came of age there was nothing left. In the old days there was not a trustee. If a person dies, that is it, your uncle takes it and eats it up. If he says, "I'll put aside the child's share," that's by his choice. If he doesn't put it aside but eats it himself, when you are old enough to understand what's going on and look for the inheritance, there's nothing left. He has already devoured it. What will you do to him? You can't sue him, you can do nothing at all.[1] The British were the ones who came to take care of children's wealth, to hold it in trust.

Bi Hindi had an *mzalia*, [a person of slave descent born in he household]. She loved him like her own child. He was called Saidi.[2] She gave him a farm and two slaves, Tumekani and Majaliwa.

Bi Izhe wa Mwenzagu was the child of Bi Hindi's sister by the same mother.[3] Bi Hindi gave her a farm. This farm is still there, on the Port Reitz road, the corner of Port Reitz.

She gave a big farm to her alone, and she gave her some slaves. She gave her Hatimjawe, Twafuateje, Afua, Heri, Kaulimwambi, Tumekani, and Faraji.

Now, the older woman [Bi Hindi] lived on and then died. After she died and was buried, everyone took their portion. Bi Izhe's farm sat and finally was mortgaged to the Liwali [Salim bin Khalfan]; it was lost to the Liwali and sold by him, so he got his money back. Salim bin Khalfan was very wealthy.[4] When he first came here, he wasn't rich. He came here trading brown cloth, and ended up becoming appointed to the position of Liwali. He brought cloth from Muscat, so whoever wanted the cloth borrowed from the Liwali. And if they haven't paid and they have a plot of ground, he takes it instead of money, even if it was for building a house. Back then it was twelve rupees for a whole plot. So, he takes the cloth, it is four to six rupees or more. You will hear, "Ah Liwali, I have no money. Here, take my plot of land instead." It's all right. What's twelve rupees? So, the Liwali takes it. Farms, the same way. Farms were sold for forty rupees. Back then it wasn't shillings, it was rupees. So the Liwali mortgaged it, gave people the money, and so on until every place was his. At Malindi, the Liwali had a passel of farms. One whole side of Lamu is his, all of Mombasa, Zanzibar too.

Bi Hindi's Slaves: Tosha, Big Hamisi, and Little Hamisi

Tosha was a Digo.[5] She didn't marry and had no children. As Bi Hindi's slave, her work was to go to Digo country. The Digo used to sell foodstuffs near Chete where there was a market. Tosha was told, "Sleep in Chete tonight and tomorrow buy food." People brought peanuts, cashews, pigeon peas, and mushrooms. At that time the Digo were simpletons. They sold things cheap. Tosha bought things, filled her basket, and returned home. Once home she didn't sell the foods. There's a special storage area built with a rack. She put the peanuts in their place, the pigeon peas in their place, the beans in their place--everything was in its place, except cassava. That was cooked because it couldn't be kept.

Big Hamisi ferried at Likoni; Little Hamisi ferried at Makupa. People crossed the water by boat, like at Likoni now. Big Hamisi came from Mwinyi Kitoja [Bi Hindi's second

husband]. Bi Hindi bought Little Hamisi herself. They were
only known to the household because they came for food; Bi
Hindi didn't let her slaves go hungry. Neither of them
married. They died before Bi Hindi did.

My Father's Slaves: Faida and Takosani

Bi Hindi gave my father Faida. She wrote him a deed
giving him a farm and Faida. She was a Luguru. She didn't
do any work. Bi Hindi gave her to my father and he made
her a concubine.[6] He secluded her; she did not have to go
out. She was his concubine. She had a child, but it died. So,
she lived with my father and when the child died, Faida had
no work. My father didn't live with her anymore. By our
custom, if you make a person a concubine and then want to
let her go, you should marry her off. You look for another
husband and marry her off. If she is not married because
you, her master, didn't find a husband for her, if she stays
unmarried and then gets another man, if she gets pregnant
and delivers a child, it must be yours. My father said, "I
made her a concubine, she had a child. When she delivered,
the child died." My father didn't want her again. She built a
house for herself and lived there. If there was something
happening at the main house, naturally she would come. If
there was a wedding, she would come. When it was over she
would return home. If there was a funeral, she would come
and sit through the funeral with everyone else. When it was
over, everyone would go home. Then my father found a
person named Msengesi, a slave of people from Zanzibar. He
returned and married Faida. They stayed here in town. He
didn't build a house; they rented other people's houses and
lived in them. She had no children.
    Bi Hindi bought Takosani.[7] She also gave her to my
father, but he did not make her a concubine. Takosani just
lived around here, that's all. She worked as she wished, for
example, at trading; at the end of the month she brought
money to the house. My father didn't insist on hard work. A
person stayed and worked as she liked. If she came to the
house and there was no water, she would draw some and fill
the jug. During meal preparation there was a special person
to cook. So, if Takosani happens to come by and wishes to
help, fine. Then, "I'm going home." "OK, you may go." She
did not have harsh slavery, Bi Hindi. They were treated like

children. With others--if a person wants to work for an Indian who is looking for help, she tells her, "Go, work for him." At the end of the month the Indian brings the rent for the slave.

I don't know where Takosani went [after the government freed her]. She left, saying, "I'm going into trading for myself." She had one miscarriage. She didn't have a child who lived. She was a Rabai; her husband, a Duruma slave, was named Hakuna.[8] They argued. He divorced her and she returned to her own place. Then when her husband died she returned to Duruma country. She worked for wages for the Indians. They liked to hire cooks and nannies.

Saidi and His Slaves: Majaliwa, Tumekani, Afua, Heri, Riziki, Maburuki

Saidi wasn't a slave. He was a child of the household. His mother, Mefundi, was a slave; to us she was an *mzalia*. It was her grandmother who came from their homeland. Her mother was born here and married a man named Fundi. Fundi Saidi was freeborn, but he was named Fundi Saidi because he did the jobs of a skilled worker.[9] Mefundi's mistress said, "This person is an *mzalia* two ways. His maternal grandmother came from their place and gave birth to Mefundi's mother. And a freeborn man came and married Mefundi's mother. She gave birth to Mefundi."

Among us, if a person is an *mzalia* once or twice you treat them like your own child, if you like. Some want a slave; they put them out the same as the others and use them. Others refuse, they say: two times an *mzalia* and their father is a freeborn man. But they keep the slave name because the grandmother was purchased. We say you let them free. You write, "This person is free. He is neither my slave nor anyone else's. I will not make him serve." Now you have set him or her free; he or she is a freed slave, an *mzalia* of the lineage, and is not a person to be ordered about: "Go fetch some water, bring it here." You seclude her like your own child. I don't know where Mefundi's grandmother came from; she was a Digo. Mefundi's mistress gave her the name of her younger sister, Mwatime.

Saidi lived in our home. He married but had no children. His wife was called Matari. She was a Giriama

convert.[10]   Saidi worked as a tailor; he sewed men's
embroidered kaftans.

Majaliwa was Saidi's slave.[11] He married and built a
house on Bi Izhe's farm in Saregoi. He married Mariamu,
Sharifa's slave, and had children who died. Majaliwa's father
came and gave Saidi money. He returned the money and
said, "Here is your money, Saidi. My child is not your
slave." They bought and sold mangoes for a living. He used
to give his mistress, Bi Hindi, money. When she died, Saidi
no longer accepted money from them.

Tumekani was a woman, a cook for some Indians.
When Hatimjawe was growing old, Tumekani was told,
"Leave your work. Come and cook for us, and the older
woman will help you." She wasn't married. She was sold as
a child from her home; she was a Chonyi.[12]

Twafuateje was a rural person. Her name meant "How
do we follow?" Bi Hindi had farms. They were farm people,
there in Changamwe. Afua and her child Riziki lived on one;
Twafuateje [Bi Izhe's slave] lived on another. They farmed
and raised coconut trees. They sold the coconuts and brought
the money to the house. They put the remaining coconuts in
a bag and brought them to the house for cooking. For herself
Twafuateje would grow cassava, potatoes, and banana plants.
Faraji was a young man, but he had no work. He had a sore;
he was always sickly. So, he did no work at all up to his
death.

Afua[13] was a Nyasa, she came from Nyasa country.
She lived on another farm, which was given to my father,
Saidi, and my uncle Mbaraka bin Ahmadi. The three were
given a big farm. It was Afua who lived there with her
husband Baheri and her children, a daughter, Riziki, and a
son, Maburuki.[14] Maburuki didn't do anything; he died as a
child. Both children died while Bi Hindi was alive; Heri and
his wife Afua outlived Bi Hindi.

Bi Izhe's Slaves: Hatimjawe, Twafuateje, Hanammoja, Noeza, Amina, Saada, Mafutaha, Mwasudi, and Kaulimwambi

Bi Izhe was given slaves by her mother, Bi Hindi:
Hatimjawe, Twafuateje,[15] Noeza, Hanammoja, and Amina.
There was no slavery with them. At our place slaves didn't
do hard work--a little work, that's all.

Hatimjawe? Her work was to cook in the kitchen. She
didn't work under slavery. A female, a Yao,[16] she was
granted her freedom by her mistress. She freed her, writing:
"She is not my slave. I give her her freedom. She has
served for many days, it's over, now she is a free person."
And after Bi Izhe had died, the government wanted to free
her again. Bi Izhe had already freed her. But Hatimjawe
accompanied her to places--for example, if there's somewhere
to spend the day, a wedding, Bi Izhe said, "Let's both go."
They both spent the day. If there was food and she wanted
to take some home, Hatimjawe would carry the food. But she
did not work to earn money to send home. She was just a
person who lived around the house. She cooked. She did not
marry. She was purchased as an adult. She was married
where she came from; when she came here she didn't marry
again. She got her freedom. Where would she stay? She
was an older woman. When Bi Izhe died she just sat, and
then she too died. Who would she cook for? Bi Hindi had
died, Bi Izhe died. She stayed with a friend, a slave from the
same household, Faida. She died there at Faida's house.

Hanammoja was a Kamba[17] woman. She worked for
the Indians for wages at Haji Muhamad's, cooking for the
children of the household. The Indians had a shop in the
house, but she was just a cook in the household. Hanammoja
had no children. She too was given to Bi Izhe by her mother.
She died before Bi Hindi.

Noeza[18] was a cook for the grandfather of those folks
who sell *leso*,[19] Abdala Kaderina's people. It was she who
was the grandfather's cook until she died at our house. When
she died I had already married and had a child. She was
purchased as an adult; she was brought from Ngindo
territory.[20] She was a female from the tribe of those who
pierce; I don't know the name of their tribe.

Bi Hindi gave Amina to her child Bi Izhe. Amina was
married twice, first to Fundi Uledi, a Zanzibari and a builder
of stone houses. Then she was divorced and married to a
fellow Nyamwezi. He married her, then died, and she was in
mourning.[21] She had no children. She cooked for a Khoja[22]
Indian family, Jafu, in Changamwe.

Saada worked for Indians too; she cooked for some
Bohoras.[23] As she wished, she came to her mistress and
said, "I received this money. Take it." But she [Bi Izhe]
didn't say to her, "Give me the money, my slave." She did it

herself knowing, "This is my mistress. If I get sick, I will be
here. If anything happens, she is here." So, she used to
come to the mistress, "Here's some money. Divide it; let's
divide it." Her mistress divides it. She gives her her share
and takes her own. She doesn't take it all, she must give
some of it to the one who did the work. Why? To encourage
her. It wasn't the kind of slavery where she would go and
say, "Hey, give me the money you've made." In our home,
slavery wasn't harsh. Saada was a Duruma.[24] She had a
husband who divorced her. Saada had her own house.

Mafutaha was a Chonyi.[25] He married a woman
named Maiki, who had no children. Mafutaha worked
pushing a rickshaw. At one time Europeans moved by means
of that rickshaw. By means of a hand-pulled rickshaw, he
took Europeans to Kilindini[26] and anywhere else they
wanted to go. Bi Hindi gave him to her child Bi Izhe.

Mwasudi was also a Chonyi. He was Bi Izhe's, her
possession. She wasn't given him by her mother; he was her
own wealth, and Mafutaha, Saada, all were her own slaves.
They were bought with her own money; that is, her husband
purchased them for her.[27] Mwasudi traveled around. He
would go upcountry and work as a porter. The Europeans
looked for porters. As porters, they walked in single file,
traveling upcountry by foot. Nairobi had no vehicles, so they
did it this way. He did occasional work and brought his
money to his mistress, Bi Hindi's child. He married a woman
called Sikukuu and had two children who died. He divorced
her, and then he married Tanao and had Asmini. Then he
divorced her and married Kishindo's mother.[28]

Saada, Mafutaha, and Mwasudi were not given their
freedom by the government. They just died. Mwasudi got
lost. No one knows to this day what route he took. His
children, those two girls, were married; then he, their father,
left. Where he went is unknown. His children looked for
him, but they did not know where he last was. Mafutaha
died. He didn't die here, he traveled and died elsewhere, I
don't know where.

Kaulimwambi was just a person from around here who
was a servant. The name Kaulimwambi means "slanderer,"
like saying "bad expression." Someone says, "Ah, that
person uses bad words." Among us slaves' names are
riddles. Kaulimwambi ran away from here; he went to
Zanzibar and died right there. He was male, from the tribe

of Africans who lived near Dar es Salaam, the uncivilized
people of Dar, a Nindi. The Nindi pierce the upper lip--the
Mahia,[29] Nindi, Nyasa, Yao. Some pierce a big hole, some
little. But they all pierce here [on the lip]--those who pierce
are the Nindi, Yao, Nyasa, Mwera, the people around Dar es
Salaam and the Nyasa area. Those people aren't Africans
from around here, they're the Zanzibar Africans. The Mahia
too are Zanzibar Africans. During the British war when they
saw people, they hid [the lip]; they were ashamed because
their whole lip was torn.

Mbaraka bin Ahmadi's Slaves: Mtenzi and Hidaya

Mbaraka bin Ahmadi, Bi Hindi gave Mtenzi and Hidaya
to him.[30] Mtenzi was with his mother, Mefaida. Mtenzi's
sister was Faida, by the same mother but different fathers. I
don't know Faida's father, but Mtenzi's father was named
Baraka. The same tribe . . . what are they? . . . the
Kami.[31] Their mother was a Kami. Mtenzi was a boy and
was born here. He only did children's work. Children could
collect mangoes from the farms and sold them in town. They
went and sold them and brought the six cents to the house.
Mtenzi came, gave six cents to his mistress, and she told him,
"Go and buy something for yourself." She never took the
money and said, "I will rob you because you are slaves." No.
When his mistress died, he did his work and did not return to
the house. He gave his money to no one. He and his sister
Faida and his mother lived together. That mother lived in
the household until her mistress Bi Hindi died; when she died,
she went to her daughter Faida's. She lived with Faida until
she died there. She was an old woman, who could look after
her at Bi Hindi's?[32]

Hidaya Mosque is located near the Marembo Mosque.
That mosque was built by Hidaya. She had several houses,
two houses with their contents and their plots, which she
sold. She didn't finish building the mosque. Then some
Indians came, formed an association, and finished it. But the
name is that of the person who began the mosque. She got
her freedom from Makutubu;[33] Bi Hindi didn't free her. She
was in business for herself after slavery. First she sold palm
wine. People told her that she was engaging in forbidden
work; palm wine is forbidden in Islam. So she stopped. Then
she built more houses with her money, rented these, and put

the money away. Then she sold them and had only that one
house to rent. She sold it to build the mosque but couldn't
complete it. After that she had no more money. She died,
the Indians came along. The Indians decided to take up a
collection among the rich people and finished the mosque.
    She was a Chagga.[34] She had no work. She married a
Zanzibari; then he divorced her. She had no children. She
didn't stay at the house; she lived outside. But at the end of
the month she brought her money. On her own she said to
her mistress, "Every month I'll bring you two rupees. I'll go
about my own business." Her mistress said, "Fine." At the
end of the month, she brought two rupees and went home.
Then after awhile, there was no more paying money. They
refused. If there is work to do, they are told, "Tell everyone
that yesterday someone died here," and they all come. They
will help at the funeral. When it is over, everyone goes
home. The owners no longer want to charge them money.
They say, "These are people who have been with us for a
long time, and I give my child some of them. Now we're just
living together. We want to take care of each other, that's
all." At our home there wasn't harsh slavery.

Baadadhiki

    Baadadhiki[35] was a Yao woman. When my
grandmother died, she left Mbaraka bin Ahmadi as a very
young infant. So, Bi Hindi, my grandmother's sister, told
Baadadhiki, "Raise him, I do not want to treat you like a
slave anymore. This is your only work as a slave." So she
raised my uncle. Then my younger brother was born, and
she raised him too. She raised Jumaa and my uncle
Mbaraka. She was our nanny and our fathers' up to my
siblings and me. She wasn't freed by the government; she
was just left, since she was a nanny, that's all. She had no
other work under slavery--she didn't farm, she didn't wash
pots, she didn't fetch water, she did nothing else. Her work
was to look after children, that's it. Her mistress told her,
"There is no work, childcare is enough. It isn't right to use
her for other hard work." She stayed with us until she died.
We buried her ourselves because she was our mother. She
was married; her husband was called Mponda, a Yao, a slave
of Bin Hashili named Bwana Mwaka. She and her husband
lived at the house. She was given her place on one side to

live, because her mistress gave it to her out of respect for
raising my brother and my uncle. She told her, "Use your
money yourself, don't give it to me." She had no children.

Abolition

The government wanted no more slavery; it wanted to
eliminate it. So it recorded all as freed slaves. All of them:
Hidaya, Takosani, Faida, Twafuateje, Faraji, and Mtenzi.
They got their freedom when she, the mistress, had already
died; the government took them and asked, "Where are Bi
Hindi's slaves?" They were all counted; some had died, those
who were alive were all freed by the government. But they
were grateful to us just the same. Among us, if they are
sick, we look after them. The slaves that the Makutubu
wanted--the Nyasa, Nindi, Luguru, Kami, Zaramo, Ngindo--
the Europeans, Makutubu, declared these to be slaves. That
is, people came with guns and everything, they fought wars,
and captured those slaves. But those slaves such as the
Digo, Duruma: "I [the Makutubu] cannot pay for them, they
aren't slaves. They were just taken in, that's all."

Among those people, the Digo--if you hear about Digo-
style slavery--it's not that a person comes and sells his or her
child. No. Say you have a brother. Now your brother goes
and steals somebody's child. He takes the child, and they
want compensation. Now you are poor, you have no money.
You tell your brother, "Take your nephew, when you get
somewhere, sell him, get some money and repay the people's
money." This is the origin of the Nyikas' slavery, all the
people from around here, those people from our part of
Africa, all of them. This is the only way they were sold. He
has taken someone's child, he has no money. They catch him
and will imprison him. His sister gives her child and tells
him to sell him to get money from that master. When they
are stolen, a Digo's child is captured and the parent is there,
but he doesn't dare to follow. He is scared. He feels, "I too
will be captured." These people long ago were stupid. That
is why their children were enslaved. To save yourself, that's
the origin of the Nyika slaves, the Digo.

When I lived at Bibi wa Shafi, servitude had been
eliminated, except for the case of a person who wanted to
work, like Takosani. She was like my mother, so in the
morning she would come and sweep for me. She lived in her

own rented house. In the morning she came to sweep for me, she drew water for me, she cooked food for me. That's it, children have been born there, and she has raised them and made them like her own. You can't come and tell her, "Do this." No, she will do as she wishes. And if you have a chance to buy some clothes, you give them to her. It's only friendship, not slavery, but she is as your friend. Once the British had come you didn't dare to call a person a slave. Mama, that's all. You send her on errands, she is useful to you if she wants to be herself, out of her own kindness. If she is kind, she will feel, "I wasn't treated badly there, I had no troubles. I don't want to stop greeting people from our home. And I raised those children." So, she will come by and greet you, and if you have a problem she will look after you. If she has gotten something of special value, she thinks, "I will bring it to my child, there." And if you have no supplies, but you have money, you say, "Mama, buy sugar so you can drink tea." During our time we didn't have slaves, they were our mothers and friends, that's all. The real period of slavery happened before us.

Childhood

Uganda Railroad

My uncle Muhamadi bu Rashidi's first job was there at
Kilindini as an overseer of the builders. It was Swahilis and
Panjabis who did it, and those called Hindoko, with pointed
caps. And the Panjabis and the Hindeo--I don't know their
tribe, they were just called the Hindeo.[1] They installed
Kilindini. On Saturday my mother (my uncle's wife) and I
went. She said to me, "Let's go to Kilindini." So we went; I
was just a youngster, but not a child who couldn't
understand. I was at the age of comprehension, but I hadn't
reached puberty. My breasts hadn't grown, but I was old
enough to remember.

They were given half a sack of rice and half a sack of
flour, or one frasila[2] of flour and half a sack of rice, and half
a frasila of sugar, and a quarter frasila of lentils, and shark,
spices for sauce, salt, pepper, all spices and wheat flour too,
and ghee--a tin for two people. Muhamadi Bu Rashidi was
the one who went to work there. They were paid in lots of
rations and small wages. They were given twenty-five
rupees, that is, fifty shillings, but lots of food. The money
wasn't used much. He worked from Kilindini, up to the
Makupa Bridge; I don't know if they have removed the pillars
now. That is, my eyes don't see--that bridge is old. They laid
the road there, they poured gravel. They continued until
Changamwe. The people from there were put to work; they
made the road the same way up to Rabai, Mazera. They
returned the Changamwe people and signed up the folks from
Mazera. The Mazera people were used until they reached

Mackinnon Road. Isn't that the *sharifu*'s grave?

They went, and what do you know, there was a Panjabi
sharifu. Now they were building the road there at Mackinnon
Road. As they made it, that *sharifu* and the people put
stones in a container and hoisted them to their heads. All the
Panjabis lifted this gravel, and their bosses, the Europeans,
supervised. Now, that *sharifu* lifted the tray and put it on his
head, but it didn't rest there. He didn't hold it with his
hands. You could see he took it, but his head didn't touch it
and his hands didn't hold it. The tray hovered there until he
reached the place where he put it down and stooped to pick
up more. The Europeans saw this. One of them came and
watched and said, "Hey, wait, be quiet. Stop your work."
He asked him, "What's your ancestry? Everyone is using
their heads, they do it that way--they carry it on their heads
and their hands grab the tray of gravel. Why don't you hold
on to it?" He said, "I hold it." He told him, "No." Then he
said, "OK, back to work." He took it the same way; the tray
didn't rest on his head and his hands didn't grasp the tray. It
floated above until he reached the place where he poured it
out. The European said, "I ask you all, what tribe is that
man? I have never seen a person hold a thing like that. Are
you a ghost or what?" The other Indians said, "He is a
sharifu." "What is a *sharifu*?" He was told, "He is a *sharifu*.
They are the Prophet's tribe, an important tribe." He was
told, "Stop this. Don't work and you will get your wages."
He was told, "They are never asked to do this kind of work.
He came, he followed the people and he is poor, he was
looking for work." He was put in the job of supervising. He
was told, "Sit, supervise, oversee those who are working."
So, he stayed there until he died. When he died he was
buried there at Mackinnon Road. And now, this month,
people go there to read Maulidi at his grave at Mackinnon
Road because of that Panjabi *sharifu*.

After this work, Muhamadi bin Rashidi went to his place
in Chonyi, among those Nyika, the Chonyi. He broke up
coconuts and sold dried coconuts that were used for making
oil. He placed people there in the forest; there was still
permission to cut down trees. He hired them to cut planks.
He took the wood and sold it in the Indians' stores. He did
this work until he died. He didn't do wage labor again; he
was self-employed.

Education

I was taught at home. Our elders did not often send
female children to Koranic school. Only one or two did, not
like now. Now all children want to go to Koranic school.
People back then didn't understand or care much about it. I
was given religious instruction by my aunt Bibi Isha
Makamu. When my father died, I went to live with his elder
brother, Bwana Pemba. His wife taught me. When she could
no longer do it, Saidi[3] took over. Then, when I returned to
live with my other uncle, Mbaraka, he refused to teach me.
He worked at his business, and so I didn't have anyone to
teach me. I wasn't sent to the Koranic school; they didn't
want to send me there. You were taught to pray; you had to
be taught to pray as a child. But people thought, "If she
knows how to write, she will write letters to men." We are
people who were made into fools; they made us idiots. Those
people like Suleima, you know, they went to Koranic school to
study. They read the Koran till they completed it, then they
went to school. When the British came they didn't want
children to go to school until they studied Arabic, until they
had finished the Koran. Then you should send them to
school. If you sent a young child, they would be returned.

There was a *madrasa* here at Konzi Mosque, Mwalimu
Ghazali's school.[4] He died and Muhamad Kassim took over.
Our children studied there, even Fatu [Zuena's daughter] and
her cousin, her mother's niece. Fatu studied and then worked
there. Many people sent their children. The rural people,
they had problems. But here in Mombasa there was a big
school and teachers. One teacher is still there; her husband
Mwalimu Ghazali died. Her name is Kimwana wa Adam
Musa; and another named Bahia. Zuena's cousin taught
here. Many taught here. As in Zanzibar, the male and
female teachers are separate.

Maulidi

In the old days one would have to read a Maulidi[5] for
the Prophet's birthday in this month. But now who will read?
The Christians, Europeans, they aren't Muslims. They don't
read Maulidi now. They used to read Maulidi. There was
lots of food and soda and everything. There was one Arab,
from Aden. He brought a trunk full of soda, and Indian

delicacies; he brought every kind of food. The European teachers sat during the reading. During the time to stand and pray, the teachers were told, "You too should stand." They took their *leso* and covered themselves, because it wasn't good for a person to remain uncovered. Miss Scott, Miss Banji, and Miss Donald wore appropriate clothes.[6] During the speech, Shuweha translated for them, "Muhamad is so, the leader of the Muslims," and they listened. She told them about religious matters. But we don't want to listen to their speeches. When they speak in their churches we do not stand, nor do we go there. For us it is very bad to listen to their sermons. Among us, we speak carefully if they are listening, because if people are open, they will come to love Islam. We don't hide our religion, but we don't want to listen to them.

Whoever wishes reads Maulidi at home. I too read it from Thursday to Thursday, but not here. I read it in the mosque, those people's mosque. I send money. Then each Thursday the teacher and his children read there, in my name.

At the mosque during this month, the seventh month, there will be a big celebration and many people--people from Jomvu, people from Magosi, people from Kutani. In Kisauni too there are many Maulidi. In Mwandoni too, Kisauni, Bamburi at Kiambeni there are Maulidi, at Mto wa Panga, Upanga, and here at the Nuru Mosque in Changamwe it has already been read. At the Nuru Mosque over there in Bondeni, not yet; and that mosque there. . . . They all read the Maulidi. Musa Mosque in Majengo, Sakina Mosque (an Indian woman was named Sakina). Musa Mosque is before that, and bigger. Maulidi is also read at Sakina Mosque, and at the Makadara Mosque every day. Now that ground has been destroyed; it was a continuous space. The British government did not raze any place where religion was practiced. They left it just like that, a continuous ground, the government and the mosque. And the Baluchis then built another mosque there. So, all the people come to that space for the big Maulidi of the twenty-seventh of the month, the end of the sixth month; the final Maulidi is there. People from Changamwe, Kisauni, Mtongwe, Likoni--everyone comes to the Maulidi.

New Year's Day

In the old days on New Year's Day[7] people went to bathe in the ocean early in the morning. They stay up all night dancing, and early in the morning they go to bathe. Children who read the Koran spend the whole night with their teacher. In the morning they take their slates to go and wash in the ocean. They scrub them at the Mbaraki beach there at Likoni. They wash their boards and bathe until they have dried. Now the teacher writes down the names of all those in his class. The girls don't go to the beach. They bathe on another side; they do not mix. These days children just bathe in their houses. In the morning they all bathe. A person with new clothes will wear them. If tomorrow is New Year's Day, today a cow will be bought.[8] That cow is the town's sacrifice, because of devils, etc. The cow is paraded around, and they read certain verses from the Koran. They read verses while they parade the cow around until they reach the beach at Nyali Bridge. After being paraded, it is slaughtered there at the beach. That meat is distributed right there. It doesn't enter the city. And bread, etc., people eat right there. It's a sacrifice for the city. People bathe, and when they're done they return. But people nowadays slaughter the animal; the meat is taken back home. That's not right, because that sacrifice is supposed to dispose of evil spirits into the ocean to eliminate the ritual pollution and sickness. The city will be invaded by some epidemic this time. This cow should be eaten right there. After it's eaten, everything is thrown into the ocean. Nowadays you don't see people because they're in the hospital all day long. There is no medicine. All the evil has been brought back into the city.

There is this Sheik Mvita.[9] That *gungu* dance is the dance of the people who mixed with that sheik. They don't dance anywhere except at Sheik Mvita's grave. On New Year's at 6:00 a.m. people dance *gungu* at Sheik Mvita's. When it strikes 7:00 a.m., people return. Other people, the Wamiji, come to watch. Those who dance are only certain women, but any man can dance. They dance in pairs, one on this side, one on the other. When one gives up the sword, the other takes it and dances with it. It is the women of the Nine Tribes who have a part of that dance. They are the ones who go and dance. They are called the Kilifi.[10] Kilifi is a district of Old Town--there is Mjua Kale, and at the end of Mjua

Kale, there is Kilifi. The people who live there are called the
Kilifi. I didn't go to Sheik Mvita near the beach, not even one
day, from when I was young until I was an adult. I didn't go
see it. I just didn't want to. It's not necessary; it's for
whoever wants to go.

Wamiji

You know who the Wamiji[11] were? *Umiji* is like having
a meeting, a gathering. We all get together. We all hold a
particular dance. If you like you enter that club. Now those
people dance; they "measure rice"; they slaughter a cow if
there is a wedding. So, they are called Wamiji. The people of
the city who do it make their own society, to show off the
Mmiji. This person is an Mmiji. They have four, five, or six
sacks of rice. They "measure rice" and divide it among
themselves. If you don't do it, you don't get any in return.

Seclusion

When I myself was born it was the period of the *shiraa*,
there were no *buibui*. Here we called it the *ramba*, a cloth
like a tarpaulin to cover a steamship. It was a large cloth; it
came from here to here, and slaves surrounded the cloth
around the outside. On this side they went around and came
around this way. All of us women were inside in the middle.
Even our legs should not be seen by men. That was the time
of those like Bi Hindi and Bi Izhe. *Buibui* came when I had
married. The Shihiris brought the *buibui*. And people from
Lamu sewed *shiraa* like ours. They sewed them so that a
person could wear one alone and be on her way.

My grandmother told Baadadhiki, "Bring Kaje so she
can come and spend the day." She would be given a big cloth
and another like the one I'm wearing. She was told, "She
shouldn't go by foot. Put her on your back." She would put
me on her back and tie me with a cloth and cover me with
that cloth. She would take that big cloth and cover me from
head to foot, covering my face. My feet shouldn't be seen by
people. She was told, "Don't go by way of the streets, so that
she would be seen by people. Go by the side paths, by the
gullies," until I reached our place at Bi Hindi's there by
Shikeli Mosque.

Ah, in the past all those like Suleima's family [the

Mazrui] did not have permission to go outside. She didn't have permission to be seen by a man, other than her brother and father. She didn't have permission to go to the store. Now these girls: if I have money, or her mother does, she will tell her to go buy me some clothes. She will go. They don't fear other people. The reason is school, studying at school. Women no longer stay inside. But we stayed inside, our children stayed inside. Suleima's grandmother Ma Zuena stayed inside until she was married. Up until she gave birth to Suleima's mother and her uncle, she had not come out. Her door was closed. Her husband will knock when he comes. She opens it, he enters. Now these girls: today they marry; tomorrow if you go to look at your bride, she has gone out with her husband to the movies. Long ago it was a great shame to be seen outside.

Those who lived on farms stayed indoors the same way. But there it isn't like here. On the farm if she has already married she goes out, if she hasn't got a person to draw water for her. There were no running water faucets; the water was far away--in wells at Magosi, Hodi, Gome, Tangai, Ziwani there by today's refinery. So, when a person goes out to draw water, she covers herself with a cloth. If there is a person or someone her elder, they will bring her water. She cannot be seen outside at the well. Or if someone calls "Hello" at the door who isn't your kin, you run away. Another person answers the call. "Is Mr. So-and-So here?" He isn't. He asks for her husband. "He isn't there." "If he comes, tell him so-and-so has come." He tells him this and that. That wife doesn't make herself visible to the one who is knocking.

I never saw dancing even once; my grandmother didn't want me to go to the dances. I don't know why. She said, "I don't want my grandchild being seen about everywhere." She and I used to sit together. When I went there, I was spoiled. There I wasn't beaten, I wasn't denied anything, nothing was done to me at Bi Hindi's. Unless I came here and did something wrong, then I would be beaten. Among us, even if women came to visit, they didn't see us. If a woman came who was not one of us, who is just someone who came to visit Bi Hindi, for sure you would be told, "Go, hide yourself in the kitchen so you won't be seen." People were trying to get a glimpse of children's faces. If a person wants to marry someone whom he doesn't know, he searches out

that person and plays a trick on her to make her show
herself. Now that potential husband, he had to enlist a
person, an adult like me. He would tell her, "I like so-and-
so's child. But I don't know her. What's she like?" Now,
that adult is the one who enters the house. She will go, "Ah,
Suleima, give me some water." That groom-to-be has hidden
himself inside a nearby house at night. He will catch a
glimpse of the young girl. Now after a while he returns, she
will tell him, "Did you see her?" He will tell the adult
woman, "I have seen her, I want her. Tell her I want her."
She will take the proposal to the girl's father. They send
word; they receive the money; they set the date of the
wedding.

But these days all people are African. There are no
customs, there is no Arab, no Twelve Tribes, no Nine Tribes,
all are African. If a person goes to school and returns, she
gets together with a man whom she wants to marry her. She
will talk to him first. They will say in their English, "I want
me, yes?"[12] Isn't it like this? So the woman will tell him,
"Go to our house." He will come and speak with her father.
He will send someone to sit with the father and say, "I want
your daughter."

Back then, only your father, and your brother, and your
mother's brother and father's brother are allowed to see
you.[13] But a man you don't know except that you know he
is so-and-so who lives in that house, he can't see your face.
It's shameful to see you. If there's a wedding, a woman goes
to the wedding; if there's a funeral, she'll go to the funeral.
But a child wouldn't go to the store. Even a married woman
didn't go. Even until now Zuena does not know the stores,
and she's not ancient. She's a contemporary person. My
first child and she are the same age. But still she hasn't
gotten used to going to the market to buy things. She stayed
inside with Fatu's father, her first husband. She didn't go
out until her other husband died. Now that I can't see and I
can't go, now Zuena goes to the stores, these stores here.
She doesn't know the stores out in the country. If there were
a servant, they would go.

All I lack are the stores of Europe, and Bombay, and
Pakistan, I don't know these. But which stores shouldn't I
know? In town? A person who was born inside the city? I
know the whole city; there's not a store I don't know. Only
recently have I gone out-- since I was a mature woman, once

I had no husband, nothing. I didn't go earlier, not even to a store near the house. I couldn't go out, I was a young girl, how could I go out as a teenager? I stayed inside, I didn't go to market. My grandmother went to the stores, she bought everything. If I wanted clothes, my grandmother had an Indian benefactor there at the market. She went there and told him, "Give me *leso*. Kaje wants clothes," and would take them. I would take those I wanted; the remainder would be returned. But since I'm over the hill, I go to the shops unveiled. I don't listen to anybody or anything. Except for the Mackinnon Market,[14] I didn't enter there. I couldn't enter the market; my grandmother, an old woman, went there. If I want sugar, anything--I enter all those places, the Shihiris'. But that meat market? No. Not even the fish market at Forodhani. Even now, if I could see the market itself, I couldn't enter it. I would be seen, "Ah! Kaje, you are entering the market!" A very old woman can enter. Like me, now, if I could see, now I could go in. Whom would I run away from? Who is there still around? There is nobody here anymore. Where are those gentlemen to be avoided?

Husbands and Children

Marriage

With us, long ago, if a man has come for you and wants you, you are not told about it. You can't refuse; you don't dare refuse. In those days would you dare to speak up to your father? He knows this man, and this man meets your social standard. The second time, your father will come and tell you, "Daughter, your husband has divorced you. Another has come, do you want him?" "Ah, yes, I want him." Or, "Ah, father, I don't want him. I don't yet want to marry." "All right, daughter, if you don't want to."

My first husband was named Muhamadi wa Mwenye Haji wa Ngao. He was from my family. He was related; his maternal grandfather and my maternal grandfather were brothers. Muhamadi was in business. He didn't work for a European or an Indian. He sent people to the forest to cut wood, which he took to the customs house and sold.

I had just been married by my first husband when people were called to be given their freedom. Bi Hindi had died. We lived at Saregoi, where we had a house that was later torn down. We lived in that house with my grandmother who raised me, Mwana Mjomvu. She built her house and gave it to me. She divided it--it was very large. One part she gave to her son, and the other part to me. When it came to be torn down, Muhamadi had already divorced me.

Muhamadi and I didn't stay together many years. We were together till my first child. The child died, then we sued each other at the Sheik's. I sued him. He wasn't doing any work. I asked him, "Now that you aren't doing any work, what do you expect?" And when he did do some work, his mother came and secretly told him, "Give me that money." She took it away. Then he ate at his brother's house, and his mother followed him and ate there too. He took me to his house and just abandoned me. I left. He had a slave named Tabia.[1] She asked me, "What's going on?" I told her, "I wasn't given anything." She said, "I'm going to cook some rice quickly. I will bring it to you." She cooked it fast, without the sauce. She told me, "Don't make sauce. I will broil a kingfish." So, quickly she cooked and broiled the kingfish. I came and ate; I finished and swept away the crumbs that had spilled. I wiped away everything and sat. They finished eating and came back.

I didn't know the streets outside. My job was to be in purdah. Tabia told me, "Run and come to my place and I will take you to your home." In the evening, they went to eat dinner. I closed the door. I told the neighbor, "Take this key." I gave them the key. They asked me, "Where are you going?" "I'm going to the toilet there at Bi Mkubwa's," where they had gone to eat. I passed quickly and came to Mwembe Tayari. I was looking for our house; I didn't know it. I saw someone and asked her, "Which house is Mashtara's?" She told me, "There it is." "Ah! What do you know, I have arrived at our house." When I got there and knocked, my brother came upon me. He was coming from the mosque. He said to me, "Why are you here?" I told him, "I have run away." "Why aren't you going inside?" I knocked. When I knocked, my grandmother saw me and said to me, "I can't keep you. You are someone else's wife. Go back where you came from, or go to the sheik. Do not come into my house. Since you are someone's wife, I will be sued." My brother took my hand and said to me, "Let's go."[2] We went to Abu's father [Sheik Suleiman bin Ali Mazrui]. I went there and he said to me, "My child, I'm not the sheik who judges cases between a husband and wife. That is Sheik Muhamadi." Sheik Muhamadi told me, "Go back to your husband and sleep there." I told him, "I'm not going, Sheik." He said to me, "Then go to his brother's." I said, "OK." I went to his brother's and slept there. My husband didn't go sleep at home, he followed me. He sweared at me and I cursed at him. We fought the whole night. In the morning when I could see the streets, I went home. Baadadhiki was

there. I told Baadadhiki, "Take me to Sheik Muhamadi bin
Kassim." She took me.

The case was decided so that he had to give me food
every day. And he was told, "Give her some money." At
that time money was made from copper. He was told,
"Every day give her twenty-five cents." After three days, he
ran away. When he ran away, I sent a report to the Sheik.
I sent my uncle. He told him, "I've come for the money."
The Sheik said, "He hasn't come for two days." When
Muhamadi came to answer me, I opened the door and left it
wide open. When he came he said, "Why did you leave the
door open?" I told him, "The wind is entering my stomach.
Shouldn't the door be open? I'm eating wind." "Close it." I
told him, "Don't you dare close the door." I wasn't hungry.
My grandmother would cook, and I climbed to the rooftop,
and I sat there and tied a basket with a rope and lowered it.[3]
My grandmother cooked and put the rice in it. I raised the
basket. I ate, and when I finished I lowered the plate. I
came downstairs, I sat right there at home. He didn't know I
had eaten. I told him, "I've had enough. I want to be
divorced." He divorced me. He kept me badly. My uncle
told Muhamadi, "I don't want you to keep her like this."

I had two children by Muhamadi: one, Ahmadi bin
Muhamadi; one, Fatuma binti Muhamadi.

When Muhamadi divorced me, I married Ali Muhamad.[4]
He divorced me. Why? I didn't want him, and I told him,
"Leave me, I don't want you." He married me and just sat
there. I ate at our family's house, got clothes there--what
good was being married? I told him, "Go away." And when
Ali came, he waited for rice at our house. I told him, "You
can't eat rice here. Go away. I will eat alone. I don't want
anyone else to help me." You know why? He was a
spendthrift, he gambled. That's the work he did. I told him,
"No, go gamble there. Then, go and eat at your brother's.
Don't come here to eat rice." He went away for a while and
returned. When he came back he brought his palm fronds.
With these he wove baskets for fishing. That was his work,
weaving. He used to put it in the water for one day; he
would get 100 rupees worth of fish. I didn't see even 100
cents. Suddenly I saw him coming in with his load of palm
fronds. I got up, took them, and threw them out. My
grandmother said to me, "Don't throw them away." I told
her, "Is this his house?" When he came, he wanted to put

them in the house. I said, "If you put them in here, I'll set them on fire." He took them at night, looked for a house at their place, and kept them there. In the morning he took them. I told him, "Divorce me." It was three years and he didn't give me a cent. I refused.

I went to my uncle's house at Mbuuni. I lived there with my child.[5] The child had been taken by my uncle and his wife, who were raising her. People grew millet and corn. I harvested rice there too--we made bundles of rice and corn. We poured the corn out on a drying mat that we had built. Underneath it was a fire to dry it out. We dried the rice in the sun. We winnowed it and put it in gunny sacks. After I had stayed a while, I got tired and told my uncle, "I want to go home." And my grandmother too.

I was married to Athmani wa Shemlandi. I had three children by him: Muhamadi wa Athmani, Zuena binti Athmani, and Shemlandi bin Athmani. It wasn't even a year and I got pregnant with Muhamadi. I stayed until my daughter by Muhamadi bin Haji was married. At the time when I was doing my daughter's wedding, Athmani became ill at his other wife's house.

He had a second wife; she had one child. She lived here in Makadara. I lived at my home at the Mzambarauni Well, there where the Digo sell vegetables. He sewed clothes on a sewing machine and sold them for money. There was nothing, no farm, no house. He had his handwork, that was all. If he got food to eat, he ate, that was it. And the house wasn't a rented house; it was his mother's.

He became ill and I went to see him. His wife and I quarreled. My son Muhamadi was a little child. He was about four years old. He used to sleep with his paternal grandmother. When the child wanted to go to the toilet, he told his grandmother, and his grandmother would get up, light the lantern, and take him to the toilet. That day he did a childish thing. He said, "I will go by myself." The lantern was lit, so he picked it up. Athmani's wife had hung cloth on the door like so. The child, not knowing, passed by the cloth and it caught fire. In the morning she told the child off and started saying rude things. I went and said, "What are you saying?" "Aa, your child burnt my cloth. Children like these go to the toilet by themselves. He's too spoiled, he doesn't want to do so. He comes here to burn up my clothes." I told her, "You have clothes? Tell me which are your clothes?" I

told her, "If my child has burnt any clothes. . . . When your
son buys clothes, he buys three sets. One of them I take, one
he gives to my child, and the fourth he gives to my cousin."
(My uncle's child. She wasn't married yet, I was raising
her.) I told her, "You have to wait for your mother-in-law to
get clothes. If somebody has labor pains, she goes and
assists in the birth so she can get one set of clothes as
payment for delivering the baby. She brings you one set of
clothes to wear, and you don't wear anything else until
somebody else is pregnant and is going to deliver. Do you
have clothes to talk about? Say so."[6] I tell her, "You don't
have any manners. Mind your manners with me. Goodbye.
I'm going." The husband is on her side; he's doing it just to
be nursed when he's ill. I tell him, "Look here, mind your
manners. I'm not scared of you just because you're this way.
Even if you were well, I would still tell you off. I'm not
scared of you. Say whatever you want to say." I tell him,
"You look after your illness. Don't look for things to say to
help your wife." I tell him, "What kind of a wife is she
anyway? When she doesn't have a cigarette she can't get
one until her mother-in-law goes and borrows to get her one.
How can she sit and tease me? I am going." I went away
and didn't go back again.

The children went and visited their father. They had
grown. One was three years and the other was about four
years old, Muhamadi and Shemlandi. Athmani gave him his
father's name, Shemlandi. Time went by until one day I'm
looking for the children and I don't see them. I roamed all
over as far as Mnazi Mmoja, up to Mwembe Bizari. I even
looked inside a well. "Ee, my children are lost." Coming
back on the way I saw them. "Where are you coming from?"
"We are coming from our father's place." "Who took you
there?" "We went by ourselves, we know the way." As it
turned out he died that night. It was as if they went to say
goodbye to their father. So I stayed and made *vitumbua*[7] at
night and the servant sold them. I was making *vitumbua*
when I heard somebody knocking, "*Hodi, Hodi!* You're being
called. Mr. Athmani is dead." So I went. We buried him. I
went back to my place and stayed. I observed a mourning
period of four months and ten days. When that was over I
didn't want to get married again.

He died first, then the children died. One [Fatuma] died
after she married, one died at the age of seven or eight, one

reached his fifth year, one [Zuena] died in her sixth month. The first died at eight months, Ahmad.

Childbirth

In the past we didn't give birth in the hospital; we delivered at home. The one who helped me the first time was my grandmother, my grandmother's sister named Mwana Mwungwana binti Bwana Haji. She was called if a pregnant woman went into labor. Everyone called her, like a doctor. The other times I was delivered by Bwana Athmani's mother. She knew how to deliver, and my grandmother could no longer see. She was by then an old woman and didn't go out. Bwana Athmani's mother was the midwife for three pregnancies, Athmani's children: Muhamadi, Shemlandi, and Zuena. Midwives were paid a little money. If a midwife is called because a woman is in labor, if she delivers the child, she will massage her with oil for two weeks and wash her with warm water. She will receive twenty shillings (or ten rupees, then).[8]

Your mother will take you for the first child; you return to your parents' home to give birth. For the second delivery, if you have your own home, your mother will come to look after you. If a woman leaves the hospital, she goes to her mother's for the forty-day period. For Fatu's [Zuena's daughter] first pregnancy, she gave birth here in Saregoi at Bibi wa Shafi. She was delivered by Mrs. Anthony.[9] Then Mrs. Anthony died, or I don't know, perhaps she returned home. They were all delivered by Mrs. Anthony, except for Sulaika, who was delivered at Pandya Clinic. When Fatu delivers, Zuena doesn't stay here where we live, she stays there at Fatu's home until forty days are over, then she returns here. When the child is a year old, she brings it here.

You are given clay medicines to drink for the labor pains. You rest until you are ready to give birth. You are ready, and the midwife waits for the child. She catches it to prevent the child from falling onto the bed. Others were placed on a small stool; they gave birth sitting. Myself, I couldn't sit. I was very afraid--my nature was to be afraid, so I lay down.

You rest in bed, and heat is placed for you under the bed. Then when you are finished giving birth, you go to the bathroom and hot water is splashed on you down there. Then

you bathe your whole body. Next you lie, stomach down, so
your stomach feels the heat. In the morning the midwife
massages you and feeds you, again at 1:00 p.m. and 4:00
p.m. These days you see women with their stomachs
hanging out. Doctors don't massage or bind women who have
delivered. But we took a cloth, tore it, wrapped it around the
stomach, and tucked it in. Long ago, if you saw a woman
with a stomach, she had it from before her pregnancy. But
you didn't see it as a result of a delivery. Nowadays, after
two pregnancies a woman's stomach sticks way out.

You rest for forty days, at which time you take a ritual
bath. (You bathe the entire time, but until you are well you
stay in the house.) If it's the first pregnancy you stay in
until forty days are up. You walk around the house if your
stomach has healed and you have no sores. Nowadays, if
you give birth at the Pandya Clinic or Aga Khan Hospital,
you leave after nine days. If you deliver at the Africans'
place, after three days you're told, "OK, go home." They go
home and they don't have any food--just thick porridge and
cabbage. Among us, after you give birth, soup is cooked for
you. You drink porridge in the morning, and at 10:00 or
11:00 a.m. you are given a large bowl of soup to drink and
meat to eat. In the afternoon you are massaged and a rice
gruel is cooked. (Not regular rice, a new mother can't eat
regular rice.) If you deliver at Pandya you can request your
customary food--chicken or goat soup is brought. Or, in the
morning you are given one cup of tea and a slice of bread.
You are brought from home your own kind of porridge, with
spices and unrefined sugar, for you to drink. At noon you are
brought your kind of food, at Pandya it's not forbidden. But
those who give birth at the African place are served boiled
cabbage. They put cabbage broth in porridge and drink it as
food for the new mother. How can blood be replaced this
way? You lose a lot of blood in childbirth. You need to eat
good foods so your blood can return and you can gain
strength.

During the month of Ramadhan you fast during the day
when you're pregnant. One reason not to is if you're sick
during the pregnancy; then you don't fast. Or if the
pregnancy is in the sixth, seventh, eighth month, if you fast
you feel bad and stop. But generally some people fast the
first month, or the second or third, even the fifth or sixth.
During Ramadhan the food that is served at night is good.

They will make for you sweetbread, Swahili doughnuts, good meat curry, vermicelli, cassava, and they must cook pigeon peas for you. And at night you will eat rice with curry, and all kinds of fruit--there are bananas, mangoes, papayas. If you want it, it's there to eat. After you've delivered, you fast--now you have no problems. If you have eaten for ten days, you must fast ten days in compensation.

Nowadays when a woman comes from giving birth, she looks for milk in a bottle to feed her child. The mother says, "I have no milk." In the past you nursed for two years. You nurse till the end of the year, and then the next year you nurse until the baby's birthday. The mother is told, "The child was born on this day, and that's it for the milk." It is forbidden for the child to suckle again. If you are pregnant before the child has finished, you continue to breastfeed if the milk isn't harmful. For some, if you are pregnant and nurse, the milk causes diarrhea and stomach trouble. Then it isn't offered; cow's milk is substituted. In the past goat's milk was often used. I nursed Muhamadi until I gave birth to Zuena, then they nursed together until his time was up. The milk didn't bother him while I was pregnant with Zuena. She did not finish her milk; she died.

Raising Children

If a child gets sick, what do you do? You administer Swahili medicine, for example, if they have a fever and convulsions. If they sleep this way, I will go to the bush. I know the medicine is there: *mnukauvundo [Cassia occidentalis]*. You stir it up and then you wash the child with it. You look for medicines: there is elephant feces, or *zinduna*, a substance like gum copal that you find on the beach. Or, you burn frankincense and have the child inhale the vapor. With us, children come down with *babu*.[10] If the child has *babu*, and you vaporize it with these medicines, it will improve. Nowadays, you vaporize these medicines, they don't work, and you have to take the child to the hospital where it is given an injection. There are no medicines used nowadays; only injections.

Among us, if your sister-in-law wants your child, she will take it with her. And if your mother wants the child to go with her, and if your husband's mother wants the child, she can take it with her. Even if your neighbor, like this one

here, has just given birth and I want to raise the child, I'll go
and ask for it. She will give it to me to spend the day. In the
afternoon when I take the child back, it doesn't want to go
with me until it has finished nursing. I'll stay with a male
child until he is a man. If he is grown and I'm still alive, I
will be with him until he marries. If the child is a female, she
will be married and I will help with her wedding. If I have
something, I will give it to her. So she is just like my child.
She will stay and know, "This is my mother who has raised
me." She tells her husband, "OK, let's go, take me to my
mother who has raised me so I can visit her." When she
comes she will greet you, and if she has something, she will
give it to you. If she has cloth, she will give it to you.

Circumcision

In the past boys were circumcised[11] at age four, five, or
seven. Others who wished to do a ceremony and slaughter a
cow waited till nine years of age. He was circumcised with a
celebration of dancing and parties and the slaughtering of
cattle. This was not by our laws; people wanted the chance
to have fun. Now, by our religious laws, when the child
reaches seven days or forty days he is circumcised. When
the child comes to his senses, he doesn't know what's been
done to him until he is older and he sees other boys. Then he
understands this was done to him too. But in the old days
people had to have a celebration for their children--they would
come, have a celebration, dance *matari* and *diriji*. The female
Wamiji spend the day; *vitumbua* and *maandazi* are made.
One circumciser was called Burahimu; another, Bwana wa
Pate. When he comes, he cuts the uvula too. Another,
Mwenye Matano wa Shebdau, was the leader of the Kilindini;
he's the one who used to circumcise. All were freeborn.
When he stopped his child took over; and when his child died,
his grandchildren took over.

Makungwi

Makungwi are those Nyasa. Those are the ones who
use *makungwi,* and people nowadays have taken to it. Those
Nyasa, Yao, Ngindo are the ones who dance the rituals.[12]
The people of Zanzibar have taken on the customs, freeborn
people too, because they have taken on the customs of those

people in the city, the Mahia.[13] They owned the city until
the Arabs entered and became Sultans. And those Mahia
have mixed with the Yao. I have heard about them, I didn't
see them. I heard that if a child has reached puberty, then
her mother will call an adult, a *kungwi*. "This child you
wanted, whom you said you wanted, here she is today." Now
the mother will provide a mat and cups. She will give twenty
shillings, or however many, I don't know how much she
gives. When the mother has given the things, the *kungwi*
will be given the child. Now that child will be taken by the
kungwi. Then they have a dance. They go and hit her, tease
her. She will be teased and beaten with a whip, each child
one by one. The child has no clothes; she is completely
naked. Grownup human beings go, take off their clothes, and
dance *unyago* naked. Heavy buttocks, breasts, some have
buttocks like a mortar. Some, breasts like mine, and others,
tits down to here. All the young girls are naked. And
likewise, the *makungwi* take off their clothes and dance bare-
breasted. While dancing they take off their clothes and
demonstrate the dance to those initiates. They're crazy.
They haven't much sense; they're not very smart.

One day an initiate was beaten. They left at dawn to
run with her. They met a brute; she beat them with a cane.
When they came, they said, "Oooh!" I was awake, I could
hear them. "Ohhh, the ears of someone's child have been
cut." You took someone's child and now you'll learn your
lesson. Also her earlobes had been pierced, and one of them
was cut.

Among us in the past there were no *makungwi*. Back
then a *kungwi* was a person--if a young woman has reached
puberty, then she gets an older woman who shows her the
proper ways. That's it, she has no *kungwi*. Nowadays they
buy *makungwi*. That is, *makungwi* want a lot of money.
When a person's child has married, the *kungwi* wants more
money. The *kungwi* wants money to braid her hair; she
wants money again. They are greedy now. They aren't
respectable people. Initially here, a daughter like us who is
the child of a respectable family, who is known to be freeborn,
she didn't go to the *makungwi*. Those Nyasa, Ngindo, Yao,
whoever wished it herself, just did it among themselves. But
an indigenous daughter, she was not taken to the *makungwi*.
Not at all, what shame to go and have a cloth wrapped
around her hips to dance, to be scratched with thorns. These

teachings of the *makungwi* are a problem. You must be
bathed naked, fed naked, made to roll around. Who would
want her child to go, except those people among themselves?
They were the ones who did these things. Among us it is
very bad to send children like this: children connected to
respectable people, daughters in the family, daughters of
people who have gone on pilgrimage to Mecca, children of
farm people themselves. And other rural people are like us,
they only live on farms, but they have chosen the character
of people in town.[14] These customs weren't adopted, people
don't like it. They don't like shameful, disgraceful things.
Some slaves here in town did not send their daughters, except
the people of Changamwe, those Nyasa, indeed there they
have adopted this way of life. Here in town it was only one
or two, those slaves, a person here and there. But many of
them don't like it themselves. You hear that they will be
"washed" in the freeborn manner. None of this sending them
to puberty rites to go and be troubled and beaten.

Adult Life

Lelemama

Lelemama is the dance of freeborn people. A slave didn't dare to dance the *lelemama* of the old days, of the Wamiji.[1] It's those very people from here--like Bi Hindi, my grandmother--who danced before we were born. The *lelemama* from here isn't that from Zanzibar; the *lelemama* from here is different.

Here when I was young, Kingi[2] and Kilungu competed in Kuze. Only women. The men's organization was *bwaride*.[3] They would be there every Sunday, drumming. The bands were ordered from Europe and brought there. I was a member, but not of those groups from long ago. At the beginning of Kingi and Kilungu, I had not yet married. But now it's finished here, the dances have been destroyed. I was a member of Kilungu for a short time only, then I stopped it. Before I married I didn't dance, how could I go out? Among us, if you have not married and are still a young girl, you can't go out and be seen. Now you can, but in earlier days here, it couldn't be done. And too, it was by choice, not for everyone.

The women of Kilungu dance with the men, but on the farm. They spend the day there, but the men do not enter the area--the men have their side and the women theirs. At night when it is time to return, the women move in front with the drum in between and the men in the rear. That is, there are people like us for whom it's shameful to be seen by men or to be recognized as "this is so-and-so." They competed by singing songs. The men's brass bands competed. The women

competed at dancing on the outskirts of town. They went to
Saregoi, our area; there weren't many buildings. Bibi wa
Shafi's house and ours, two or three houses, that's all.
People came there to the coconut and mango trees on the
farms. There beneath the mango trees they placed the
drums and danced. Food was cooked, people ate and spent
the day there on the outskirts of town, and the men ate on
their side at the back.

Kingi and Kilungu competed with each other. Then
came Darsudi and Darweshi. Darweshi competed with
whom? Kilungu. They sang, "A half pound hem; we're
wearing them as the Kilungu army, passing in front of
Darweshi." First they competed with Kingi, then with
Darweshi. Darsudi competed with whom? The people of
Mbaraka Alwili and Mezaidi of Darsudi. They are finished
now, those like Kinana are just rubbish. Then came those
like Kinana, Landrova, Seifu; the dances ended. Children
nowadays have no dance groups. Among themselves they
dance *chakacha* at weddings, that's all.[4]

The people of Kilungu were the ones who divided. Half
became Scotchi.[5] And Kingi themselves were scattered.
Hamisi of the Station remained, a civil servant who had his
own group. But in Kuze there is no one remaining to send
beni as a gift.[6] Bi Mwenye isn't there, not Bi Shuli, or Bi
Asha, or Ma Nyinyi, or Bibi wa Salimu. Sir Ali [Liwali Sir
Ali bin Salim] entered Scotchi's man-of-war float. People
watched through the night at Sparki. The man-of-war
started and was moved inside a truck. It was brought to the
open plot. Sir Ali rose, stood up, and in front of everyone
entered Scotchi's man-of-war. Those days I didn't like to
watch *gwaride* very much, but on Sir Ali's day, I went. He
stood up, in his brown *kanzu* and red hat, a tarbush. He
stood up in front of everyone and entered Scotchi's man-of-
war. Only Scotchi built the man-of-war. Kingi didn't dare
build one. Kilungu wanted to build one, but Sheik Nasoro
was told, "Who will you have inaugurate it? Scotchi had Sir
Ali, who will you have? Don't look for big trouble." So he
left it at that. Now, even if there were dances, we don't dare
to dance them--those trucks! Who will dance? Our children
were in *bwaride*. Now, if a child goes out, we look for him,
"Oh dear, where has he gone?"

World War One

During the German-British war my deceased daughter Fatuma was seven years old. There were two wars, the war of the Germans and the British and the war of the British and the Italians.[7] They fought among themselves there. They were told, if they fight they should fight over there in Europe. Here it just was noise. The soldiers: those Mahindoo, Mazula[8] too were brought here, lots of Europeans and British. The Germans all ran away to their place, Tanga. The British followed them to Tanga to remove them, they ran away and went to their headquarters in Mwanza. Mwanza was indeed a German town. Mwanza, Tabora, Msumbiji, among the Nyamwezi; Dar es Salaam also was theirs and their camp, full of Germans. They were chased by the British, they chased them to Mwanza and caught them there. The Germans ran away, and they were conquered.

My brother Jumaa was taken by the Carrier.[9] They went; those who died, died, those who returned, returned. Jumaa was a servant.[10] He had his European named Newly, who was sent to work with airplanes. My grandmother had a premonition; she told him, "Don't go." He replied, "I will go." But he was only hit once in reaching Taita Maktau. There is a town called Maktau. There's a large mountain there, and people were fighting for Maktau. They were killed, the Europeans and everyone, there on the road to Maktau. There was nowhere to walk but on people, just on people's bones. He said, "I was sick with fear of those people, to walk on them." When he came back, they came back for good. The European's stay in Mombasa had ended. He was fired and went back to Europe.

World War Two

During the war of the Italians and the Germans, Fatu's kin went to Zanzibar. She was young. They went to hide in Zanzibar. Her brother had then become Liwali.[11] He took her and his wife, the deceased Bi Uba. The Europeans were in the city raising a ruckus. There wasn't any war, only their commotion. So they were sent to Zanzibar. We--Zuena (her husband Ali bin Abdala was still alive)--we both were sent to Mtongwe.

Living with Zuena

I took ill and was very sick until one leg was so swollen
it couldn't touch the ground. The neighbors came and got me
and I spent the day with them. The woman, may God rest
her in peace, said, "Call her and distract her, she's feeling
bad." So it went on until I calmed down and came back to
the city again. I stayed with my brother. We rented a house
and stayed together.

Zuena's aunt and I knew each other, so I said to Zuena,
"I want to rent a room. My brother has gone to his wife's."
I rented a room and stayed there. The first month I paid
rent. The second month Zuena said to me, "I don't want any
rent." "Why not?" She said, "Aa, let's just live together. I
don't want any money." So we lived together.[12]

Weaving

I wove and sewed food covers, mats, and coverings.[13]
In the old days it was fifty cents, ten or twenty rupees, for a
mat, that's all. But toward the end we sold a dish cover for
one and one-half shillings, and a mat for forty or fifty
shillings--there isn't just one kind of mat. Whoever didn't
know how to sew, bought the craft items; whoever knew
herself would cook the fibers and sew.

There was one European woman named Bi Halisha.
She used to be accompanied by Mwinyi Fakih wa Matano, a
Changamwe from the city. My grandmother's mother, her
mother's sister, sewed covers, mats, and strips. Bi Halisha
wanted all kinds of designs of strips of plaited mats, the
beginning pieces. She bought them for two rupees. She
bought them and then took them with her to Europe. I don't
know if it was a design of a *leso* or a design of a piece of cloth
for a dress; but she took every kind of strip. And she asked,
"What do you call this?" She was told, "This is called
Peanuts, Jigija,[14] Hook, Shield." A person plaits a saying
into the big strip for wide mats, for example, "That which is
yours is mine." She put lines of poetry into that strip of
plaiting. Bi Halisha bought all the pieces like that. If a
person has a wedding, a child to be married, she must get
mats, because the houses had big sitting rooms. In a huge
room here there would be a bed and mat and mattress and its
pillows; and over here, a mat and a mattress and its pillows

and large cushions, those large ones sewn with sharp corners.

Pereira's Wife's Funeral

When his wife died, Pereira sent out invitations, five or six large bags of letters. When 4:00 came, the woman was taken and put in the coffin--I climbed up onto our house at Lango la Kuinama. But it wasn't just some people; it was a lot of people. He sent letters to all tribes, one bag for each tribe, up to the Europeans. They all came.[15] The Europeans follow in procession, and the Goans, but the Arabs turned back. That is, all the Muslims turned back. It isn't customary for us to go all the way to the cemetery. We came and Pereira saw us, that was enough.

His wife was the daughter of a Goan leader named Souza. He was the head of Goans of all occupations. Mrs. Pereira had respect for people's religions. The Pereira family lived upstairs; their door faced my place. Now, if the *mwaadhini* sounded the call to prayer and people wanted to pray, those children of hers who had returned from school imitated the *mwaadhini*. Suddenly you heard them crying; she was beating them. So one day I went and asked her, "Every day when the children have returned from school you beat them. What have they done?" She told me, "It isn't our custom to make fun of people's religion. Each person has their own religion. When your children come from the classes where they study Arabic, they see us performing our rituals but they don't tease us. But my own children, if they hear the person from your religion calling out in the mosque, that *mwaadhini*, they imitate him. Why? To make fun of people's religion. That's when I hit them. It is not our custom to poke fun at people's religion. Everyone has their own religion. It's not right to mock it." So, every day she beat her children. She said, "People who are Muslims have their religion; heathen have their religion; Europeans have their religion, and so on, with everyone. All people have their own place. But it is not good to tease another person." I told her, "But these are children, what do they know?" She told me, "If I don't train them now, they will continue to do this every day."[16]

PART II

Mishi wa Abdala

Mishi wa Abdala holding her great-grandson, 1973
Photograph by Margaret Strobel

Introduction

Mishi wa Abdala, who was born between 1900 and 1905, is in many ways a typical member of the Swahili community of Mombasa. Her grandparents were slaves brought from Mozambique. As freed slaves the family became Christians at the Freretown Mission on the mainland near Mombasa Island. Nonetheless, Ma Mishi was raised as a Muslim and grew up to be a leader in one of the groups of *makungwi* (s., *kungwi* abstract form, *ukungwi*), women who conduct life cycle rituals that are found in Mombasa and elsewhere in east Africa.

The text of Ma Mishi's life conveys something of her warmth and kindness. She has *imani*, the compassion that she finds has disappeared in interactions and relationships between people. As just one example, she raised a boy who was the son of a prostitute by some European customer. The woman asked Ma Mishi to care for him, leaving a few shillings for the first few months. She then disappeared, and Ma Mishi raised him as her own. Being both a mixed European-African child and illegitimate, the boy would have been socially stigmatized.

In the mid-1970s when these interviews were done, Ma Mishi was a vital leader in the *makungwi's* group. She lived in Kaloleni, a multiethnic neighborhood of Swahili and upcountry people on Mombasa Island that was settled in the 1920s and 1930s. She did not look her age (thanks in part to hair dye) and had sufficient energy to take care of her great-grandson while his mother worked in a nearby factory. By 1983 when Sarah Mirza visited her to reaffirm her consent for publishing the texts as presently edited, she had aged considerably and spent her days and nights in an unlighted room. Although her kindness was still evident, she had lost some of her mental agility, hence we were unable to enlarge her description of the initiation rites beyond the initial interviews. In the ten years that had passed, Ma Mishi felt that no one kept the secrets of *ukungwi* anymore, and she wished to have the songs preserved. (When the interviews were first done, Margaret Strobel wished to respect the secrecy of the rituals and did not record and translate the songs well enough to be reproduced here.) Ma Mishi died January 8, 1986.

Ma Mishi's ancestors typify people who were captured in east-central Africa and sold into slavery along the coast. It is estimated that "the slave trade of the northern section of the east African coast was in the neighborhood of 20,000 to 25,000 slaves per year in the 1860's" at the peak of the trade.[1] Ma Mishi's maternal grandparents most likely arrived in Mombasa in the 1870s, at a time when Britain was pressuring the Sultan of Zanzibar to further limit the slave trade in his realm. In the 1860s, nearly all of Zanzibar's slaves came from the Kilwa area in southern Tanzania, tapping populations into the Lake Nyasa area and drawing from northern Mozambique the Yao, Makonde, and Makua (Ma Mishi's maternal ancestors).[2] When the Sultan of Zanzibar passed a decree in 1873 banning all trade in slaves by sea, traders responded by moving them on land. The abolition of the land trade in 1876 further limited, but did not stop, the trade, witness Ma Mishi's grandparents.

Ma Mishi is not clear as to how her grandparents came to be at the Church Missionary Society (CMS) mission in Freretown, on the Kisauni mainland near Mombasa. The British tried to enforce the ban on slave trading by capturing dhows loaded with slaves. Beginning in 1875 these recaptured slaves were brought to Freretown, hopefully to become self-supporting Christians. By 1877 there were 380 freed slaves there, about 250 of them adults.[3] Founded in 1844, the mission had first languished and then developed strained relations with local slave owners who feared, with reason, that Freretown harbored runaway slaves. Kongowea, where Ma Mishi's parents took up residence later, was a freed slave community near Freretown. Thus Ma

Mishi's grandparents may have come as recaptured slaves from dhows or as runaways from local owners.

In some ways Ma Mishi's view of ethnicity in Mombasa contrasts with that of Bi Kaje. Where the latter makes careful distinctions between the Twelve Tribes and Arabs, Ma Mishi lumps the two: "They lived there and found work with some Swahilis, Arabs from here who converted them." Upon leaving the mission, Ma Mishi's parents assimilated into the heterogeneous Swahili culture of Mombasa. Although Ma Mishi is highly critical of Arab slave owners who discriminated against Africans, she expresses affection and caring for the Arab woman who raised her and gave Mishi her own mother's name.

Ma Mishi is immersed in *ukungwi*, linked through it to a network of female friends and relatives. *Ukungwi* represents for her a world view, coexistent with Islam, as much as does Bi Kaje's orientation as a Twelve Tribes woman. Ma Mishi's description of the *makungwi*'s rituals and their origins reveals the eclecticism of Swahili culture.[4] Brought by slaves to Mombasa from elsewhere in east and central Africa, these rites continue today as a subculture within Swahili society. Until recently, the slave origins of the *makungwi*'s rituals made them unpopular with freeborn descendants in Mombasa like Bi Kaje. Freeborn people did not initiate their girls collectively. Instead they were instructed individually by a *somo* about matters of menstruation and sexuality. In the past, especially, freeborn people did not call this woman a *kungwi*. However, Ma Mishi and other *makungwi* use the terms *somo* and *kungwi* interchangeably. To Ma Mishi, the rituals represent a source of pride, the instilling of proper values, not the meaningless cruelty assumed by outsiders. She notes that while some slaves and their descendants absorbed the values and customs of freeborn Swahili people, others chose to continue the practices of their ancestors.

These rites have changed, however, in being transported from the horticultural, often matrilineal societies in which they were practiced by slaves who were brought to Mombasa. The present rites include an element of Islamic ritual. Moreover, recently the magical aspects of their assumed efficacy--the transformation of the young girl into a woman-- have receded, and the function of display seems to have taken precedence. Concomitantly, puberty rituals are a less important part of the *makungwi*'s life cycle rituals today

compared with wedding dances, with which they experiment
and innovate, as Ma Mishi indicates.

In addition to revealing the mixed social origins of
Swahili culture, Ma Mishi's account also reflects its
patriarchal emphasis. Her rendition of the origins of the
makungwi's knowledge, i.e., that the founder, Nyakanga,
learned these secrets from a man, Ngariba, assigns a place of
primacy to a man in these female rituals. And she clearly
states the hierarchy of relations: Ngariba, then Nyakanga,
then the child who is initiated. (The three are identified as
Makua, Ngindo, and Yao, reflecting the diverse groups from
whom slaves were taken.) To learn the secrets, Nyakanga
runs away into the forest to Ngariba. In retiring to the
forest, she withdraws from the routine of everyday life and
society into what Victor Turner describes as a liminal state,
where the abnormal reigns and where usual time and
relationships are suspended.[5] This withdrawal is part of the
initiate's experience as well during the puberty rituals.

Despite the ritual's patriarchal bias, women themselves
form the core and are the practitioners. In a society in which
women generally do not hold political or religious office, these
roles are important sources of authority and power for
women. As we noted in Bi Kaje's description of local
celebrations, the difference between *mila* (custom) and *sheria*
(Muslim law) is relevant in examining *ukungwi*. To the
extent that *sheria* prevails, women are excluded; in the realm
of *mila* one finds more women active and in positions of real
power.[6] Thus it is not surprising to find women exhibiting
leadership and participating in significant numbers in the
makungwi's rituals. The rituals surrounding the funeral of
Ma Shea, the senior *kungwi*, indicate the importance of the
role hierarchy for these women. Somewhat confusingly,
kungwi is both a generic term for one who initiates and a
lower rank. *Nyakanga* is both a higher rank and the name of
the mythical first *kungwi*. (In the text, the rank is capitalized
and italicized; the name is capitalized and not italicized.)

Ma Mishi describes aspects of the puberty rituals. Some
of the rituals are designed to teach the *makungwi*'s secrets
and proper behavior, particularly regarding sexual matters
and one's relationship with a husband. Others require them
to perform difficult or awkward maneuvers. This feature
highlights the liminality of the initiates at this time. These
rituals do not involve clitoridectomy, a practice which Ma

Mishi condemned as the barbarity *(ushenzi)* of other cultures. In the mid-1970s wedding dances rivaled the puberty rituals in commanding the energy and enthusiasm of the *makungwi*.[7] The celebration of a wedding took place over a number of days, depending upon the wealth of the families involved and whether or not this was the first marriage for the bride. Men and women celebrated separately, as is appropriate in a Muslim society. The men's ceremony consisted of the religious vows, spoken by the groom and the bride's guardian. The men then met and celebrated by eating special foods. The groom's family and friends escorted him to the bride's house at the appropriate time for the consummation of the marriage.

The women's celebrations were more elaborate and festive. In several aspects the *makungwi* dances mirror those of freeborn people, identified as *vugo*, after the buffalo horns that were struck during them.[8] Placing a large drum inaugurated the wedding. In past times, only freeborn persons were allowed to beat the drum; the *makungwi's* drum dance broke that tradition. The *makungwi* were very proud that they wore a red sash *(bendera)*, a recent stylish innovation. Similarly, since the time of Ma Mishi's own wedding they had introduced the Stuffing Kapok into Pillows dance, which choreographed making pillows, a traditional activity that was part of preparing for the marriage of a new bride.

Not only have the *makungwi* absorbed aspects of the traditional freeborn wedding, they also form rival, competing pairs characteristic of coastal society.[9] This tradition of competition and factionalism is found in the *lelemama* and *beni* groups (Kingi and Kilungu) mentioned by Bi Kaje and in the *lelemama* groups Banu Saada and Ibinaal Watan, about which Mwana Kutani speaks. The Old Town *makungwi* of which Ma Mishi is a part are traditional rivals with *makungwi* from Majengo, the newer neighborhoods in Mombasa.

My Family

My Parents

I was born here in Mombasa in Kisauni. My mother was called Fatuma. Her name was also Metatu, Tatu's mother. (Her eldest child, who was sickly, was named Tatu.) Her special name was Nancy. She was a Christian before we were born. One sibling was named Liza, one Grace, one Edith, but all her siblings died. Only my mother remained of the four girls and of three boys named Eric, John, and Willy. Other people don't understand the name Nancy, they called her Nemsi.[1] She too was born in Kisauni. Her mother came here as a young girl, then Nancy's father married her. When they came here they were Muslims. They were captives in war; they were stolen by the Arabs. When they arrived here the leader of the church said, "They are mine," and he took Nancy. That's when they became Christians--the church they built there in Freretown. They came from Mozambique; they are Makua. Nancy's grandfather came from there too, he and her father and her mother--all three of them were Makua. Their home was Mozambique, where the people just gained independence.[2] They were married there, then Nancy's mother was brought here. My maternal grandfather was named Sudi, a name from Mozambique. Nancy's paternal grandmother was Fatuma; and her maternal grandmother was named Saada. Then they came here, studied, and were baptized by Bwana Shepherd. Nancy was the oldest.

Our father was a Zanzibari. A Christian like the others, he was named Albert. Then he and my mother converted, they were married, and we were born. He was then called Abdala, and mama, Fatuma. She sinned by having a baby by our father out of wedlock, so she was kicked out of the church.[3] They thought it was better to come here to live.

They lived there and found work with some Swahilis, Arabs from here who converted them. They found work with the Arabs, built big houses, and started farming. So they stayed there at Kongowea, not far from here. Then they had children. Aisha was born, and Tatu. (Tatu's real name was Salma, but she was called Tatu--Three--because she was born Monday--the third day.) Another, Thula, was born, and Mbaya, then we were born, our brothers Sudi, Buki, Omari. She had no trouble giving birth, she had many children. We did not bear children like she did. Then Abdala divorced her. She had children by both our father and the other man, Ramadhani--those children are much younger than we.

Abdala was a chief boy, a cook.[4] He got a transfer and went somewhere, perhaps Durban. He lived in Europe with Europeans. Nancy's work was to braid hair for money. Muhamad bin Isaa Timami's people were very rich, all the farms here around Kongowea belonged to them. Abdala bought a farm. He told Nancy, "Stay here, and the man who wants to marry you should stay here too. He should raise my children for me because I can't do it. I'm traveling all the time to work for the Europeans. Take care of things for me: it's fine. You and I have spent our time together; better you listen to him and stay here." He didn't leave her with bad will. They continued on this way with no trouble. Other people had problems when a husband divorced his wife with a big fuss. My father bought the farm there that belonged to an Arab for twelve rupees, with coconut, mango, and orange trees--every kind of a tree. When he divorced my mother he left everything for her. Then he got angry and came and sold everything, took the money, and went away.

She was married by another man named Ramadhani. He lived right there. He built his house there and lived with his children. When he wasn't there, he was traveling. If another came and married her, she would continue to stay there.

We were raised here in Kisauni. My *somo* was named Thula. She was a good friend of my mother, not a relative. Each one came from her own tribe. Thula was a person from Old Town in Mombasa, you know, the Digo, Chonyi, Giriama,

those people from here.⁵ My mother took me to Thula and
told her, "Initiate her when she reaches puberty." I was
initiated there. I was taken across the way by my mother.
And my sister, Dogo, was taken similarly to her *somo*, Fatma
Mwaita, who was the leader of Banu Saada. We were twins.
Dogo [Little] was named Saada, great-grandmother's name.
I was called "Big."

My mother was an important *kungwi* here. Among the
makungwi, once a woman is initiated, others give her girls to
initiate. Children my mother initiated are now old women.
Her *kungwi* was named Bahati, a person from Freretown just
like herself. They didn't object at the mission.⁶ There are
people who danced this very dance. Everyone who had a
child brought her to my mother, and others joined the group
as well. They danced, and this too wasn't questioned by the
Europeans at the mission. They said, "It's their business,
why should we prevent them?" They continued and the
whole thing grew. They slaughtered goats. There was one
man, Mr. Binns. He asked, "What do you want? A goat?
OK, take a goat." He, a person from the mission, took them
to Arabs and gave them a bag of rice. "Are you dancing,
Nancy?" "Yes." "OK, if you're dancing, what do you want?"
"I haven't gotten rice." He gave it to her. The missionaries
gave her a lot.

For three or four years I was raised by a rich Arab
woman from here, Bi Aziza Jeneby. They raised me right
here in Kongowea. We came to visit in town because of the
dances, but Kongowea is our home. My mother who raised
me said, "Ah, I will give her the name of my own mother,
Mishi." Bi Aziza's mother was named Mishi. There was
good will back then. People felt compassion for one another.
It didn't have to be your own child. Bi Aziza begged my
father when he returned from the Transvaal. She said, "It's
best that you give Mishi to me because there are two of them.
She can't handle it, she has her own work braiding hair.⁷
Give the child to me." My father agreed.

My Husbands and Child

My twin and I reached puberty during the First World
War. After we were initiated, we were married. We were
told airplanes would come from the sky--when we were told
this we were still girls. But it came true; we saw the

airplanes. At that time we married. My younger sister married first. She had all boys. Other men were here; Halima's father [Mbaruk Msalim] was a soldier here at their camp--a cook for the Europeans, but a soldier nonetheless.

Mbaruk Msalim was a Muslim. He asked my mother and father for permission to marry and paid the bridewealth; it wasn't free. But at that time, it wasn't that much money, about 200 shillings, that's all. Now it's 1,300 shillings. He was born in Malindi. He came here to work and then looked for women right here. He's from the Gunya, Tikuu tribe. He was senior boy, the key holder. When visitors came to the house, the lady and gentleman of the house didn't do any work. He did everything as the holder of the keys. When he came here to work, he traveled with the Europeans. When he wanted to travel, he left me here at our place and then went to Europe for two or three years. But he sent me food.

We lived here in Mombasa at Mjua Kale. There we are not strangers, that's our place near Mwana Kutani's. Even my *somo* was in the same area. She had a husband right in the same neighborhood.

I gave birth to our only child, Halima. I only had that one, she was the first and last. We lived together until she was grown, and we arranged for her marriage.

We went to Nairobi by ourselves, the two of us. After I had Halima we went to Nairobi and lived. We returned and put her in school. I wasn't important yet in *ukungwi*. I hadn't advanced enough to want to participate with the *makungwi*. I was a stranger, whom would I initiate with? If something came up, mother would send me a letter. I asked my husband for permission. He said, "Go." So I returned home and performed the dance rituals. When it was over I packed my things and came back home. There were *makungwi* in Nairobi, but now they are dead. Only a few remain.

The white woman for whom my husband worked had odd jobs here and there--to wash dresses, skirts, and underwear, and to iron.[8] Sometimes she said, "I'm going out at this or that time, Mishi." Then I would take out certain clothes of certain colors for her to wear. I used to make sixty shillings per month. She did this out of her own kindness. The lady liked me very much. She taught me to sew, to crochet, to make socks, and to do many other kinds of work. Even now, when I hold a piece of yarn, I have to knit. After

three years the Europeans returned home. We came home
for three months. When the European came back we
returned to him. We stayed for six years in Nairobi. We
were strangers there. When the European went home for
good, my husband left me. We lived in Spaki, then we built
our house in Mjua Kale. He left me in his house, then later
on he remarried after he divorced me.

He divorced me and I married another man, another
husband who was good natured. He was an Arab, a Mazrui,
Lamini. He came from Takaungu. He was kind and he
raised all my children.[9] I didn't have any by him. Even up
to now the children cry when they remember him. He was a
very good man. Mbaruk Msalim divorced me and married
another wife, but Lamini remained my husband until he died.
He died a while back.

My Work

After my husband died, I said, "Bwana Lamini is dead,
who will look after me?" So then I worked at the
Muhashamys'; I cooked there for many days until the war for
independence. My employer told me, "You must go to
Kisauni." I told him, "I can't. My child is not well.[10] If I go
to Kisauni or Bamburi, how close is that? If something
happens, who will take me home? He was going to Europe
and didn't want the job of Liwali. So I left him and and went
to cook for Moses Mohamed. It is hard to find someone to
feed you and your children. I worked, but for ordinary
people. I didn't work for classy folks anymore, just poor
people like myself, for twenty shillings, fifty shillings. And I
thought it wasn't worth it. My eyes had gone bad from the
smoke.

Living in Kaloleni

We lived in Mjua Kale. When Lamini died, his siblings
made trouble. I said, "I don't want to be killed over a house.
If you're selling it, sell it and give me what is mine." They
sold it and gave me my share. Then my child Jabu bought
this house in Kaloleni. She said, "I bought this house, but it
isn't completely finished." We built it slowly and moved in
nine years ago. Jabu is the daughter of my younger sibling,
and when she was born I took her day and night.

Puberty Rites, Weddings, and *Lelemama*

Makungwi

When a girl reaches puberty she is taken to a *somo*. You go to the *somo*. She washes you and puts cloths on you to stop the blood from reaching your other clothes. She does her best to promote modesty, and you must wash that cloth until it is white. You wear another cloth and then your *leso*. By yourself, could you know about this? You have to be taught. Then you just come to know the dances. The initiate doesn't have good manners; the dance is the way to teach manners. "That girl has bad manners. We'll make her dance." We are there when she dances, but you do that work yourself. The dance is for manners and respect.

Now there are more Muslims. There are some Christians, but not many. Many Arab girls are brought because they have no manners. They are brought to be taught manners at the dances. They used to be ashamed to come, but now girls are really bad. The men and women decide among themselves to marry. One used to get a letter of proposal, right? The bride should come and be married. But now they have no patience. That's why they are brought to the dances. They are brought and beaten. Christian children are very well mannered. Even we were taught Christian manners because our mother was Christian.

In dances these days we are more gentle. We don't act the way our mother did. They had no empathy. The initiates were really beaten. When the *makungwi* got drunk they really beat us.[1] I don't want that. I just teach. If the girl makes a mistake, I only hit her once.

And if you marry, the *somo* who initiated you teaches
you.[2] If you and your husband quarrel, she will come and
ask what's going on: "Why are you being mean to her? So
why can't you be patient? She's young; can't you see you're
older? We want to see you help her and raise her the way
you would your child. A person should care for his wife like a
child you gave birth to." So, you help a lot and she stays
with her husband.

Nyakanga and Ngariba

Kungwi herself originated these things. She knew these
things, and she knew some things about men. But her own
husband didn't know anything, and she wanted to initiate
girls. She got another husband,[3] one who knew these things,
like a circumciser. And that husband was Ngariba
(Circumciser). He cut people and circumcised them with
Nyakanga. He taught her; he told her, "Cleanse those
women; perform the women's rites." Do you know that tree
we used and the beads and everything?[4] They climbed into
the base of a big tree of that kind. That tree is used in the
dance, for the tray, the pestle and the mortar. He made her
a wooden tray, like a copper tray, but of wood. He made her
a tray and a pestle and mortar to pulverize the medicine.
That man was clever; he taught her a lot.

Ngariba was born and in the same way he had a mentor
who was circumciser. When he died, he bequeathed the work
to his child because the work had increased. Nyakanga and
Ngariba came from the Kilwa area; that's where this activity
came from. Nyakanga was a Ngindo, the man was a Makua,
and the third was a Yao, the child who wanted to be initiated.
She was given the child and she did the things to her. That
man taught her with all his heart, out of his good will. He
continued; he was the head, with Nyakanga. Nyakanga's
origin is that man Ngariba. Ngariba is above Nyakanga.
Nyakanga is a wife; Ngariba a husband.

We have these medicines that we give to children. It's
called *mbura*. That tree's name is *rihimba*. The tree is very
strong. It is used for sweeping, for mortars; it's OK for
everything except for objects that go over a fire, because it's
flammable. All these things were made from this tree, cups
too. When the head Nyakanga was receiving her orders from
her husband. It's a tree, *mbura* is its name. It's called

mzongomzongo. This tree is what they were shown to make children vomit.[5] It's the same tree as is used for the dance. It's that tree, *mzongomzongo*, but we don't call it by that name. We call it *pombe*. Nyakanga herself called it *pombe*, because it is medicine for everyone to drink. It is medicine for spirit exorcisms; people who are possessed are given this. It wasn't bad.

Puberty Rites in Mombasa

Women who were shown by their elders before them sent their children to *makungwi*. Each one paid money and was instructed. She was given a girl and initiated her. She was told to carry the initiate on her back: "Here, carry her." When the *kungwi* carried her, everything was done for the initiate, who paid money. She would go to the forest; she would go there, and she would do everything that was supposed to be done. Later, when the initiate got her own initiate, she showed her, and so it continued. When her *kungwi* died, she took over. The one who had been instructed in it took over, and so things progressed.

Every place has its own rites. Mombasa has its own *makungwi*. Dar es Salaam has its own, Tanga too. It's the same dance, with only small variations. The rites are the same.

Ma Shea's Funeral

When Ma Shea died, she was the *somo* of all of us.[6] We got together for the funeral. She was our mother who loved us. "What do you say? Will you all accept the customary gifts?" Ma Shea's successor said, "Yes, we will." Every *kungwi* gave her *somo* one set of *leso*, 4 shillings, one bottle of rose water--to all the important *Nyakanga*, like me, Tufaa, and many others. Still others, many whose *somo* had died, received it from their own initiates. And they in return each gave us 30 shillings. We collected about 820 shillings. Then we had a feast. We invited the *makungwi*, who came, ate, and left. At the time of the gift-giving, we washed the drums because their owner had died. Now what remained was the mourning period, which lasts until her eldest initiate takes the chair. There were others who were older. I'm not her initiate, I'm just her child. Mama Iko and I did not receive

her gifts, she is only our mother.[7] Mbaya will take the gifts,
or Mwana Imu, or Mishi wa Mademu--about five people.
Their leader will be Mbaya. If she doesn't know enough, Ma
Iko and I will teach her.

I have taken my mother's chair. It was taken by her
eldest initiate, Momo Kikoi. Then I took it from her. I gave
the dues to everyone and took the chair. When the time
came for someone to take the chair of my mother's initiate,
my own *somo* was still young, so I took it instead. It was
OK, because the teachings are the same. Now it is I who
transmit the knowledge; it's I who know it. I tell them, "Do
this and that," until they understand.

Some people, if their *somo* dies and they're poor, they
just "cry." They only give customary gifts for crying: fifty
shillings, three sets of *leso*, one bottle of oil, and millet. They
come and wash the drums for their *somo*. Their rank
remains the same, *Goma*. When they enter a room, the
drums cease. Many do this because their *somo* hasn't
reached the age to become a *Nyakanga*, she's still young.

Puberty Rites

The initiates are decorated in the room [see Figure 1]
where they are washed. When you enter, you see that stone
which holds down that piece of cloth for burying the seven
seeds.[8] Each seed has its own meaning. Maize stands for
the husband. Green gram is the initiate, who can give birth.
Beans represent an unclean initiate; if her period comes she
messes herself up in the process of cleaning. Bulrush millet
is also the initiate who can give birth. Rice is food that the
makungwi themselves consider better than anything else.
Sesame is uncleanliness; don't you see it is somewhat dark.
Millet is the first food the Nyakanga used to cook beer. Their
beer was made very strong. It was their first obligation. It
must be there, even if they didn't cook anything else. It's
essential to bury those seeds; they will tell you everything.

We draw designs. Nyakanga drew them because her
somo showed her how and told her, "You have to do it this
way." If you want to initiate a child, she will draw them
herself. Or, if you wish you will draw them. There has to be
someone so the initiate will know their meaning. There's
Nyakanga [#1, see Figure 2]; there's Nyakanga's husband
[#2]; there's the initiate's companion. The Ngariba is near

the moon [#5]. Men don't menstruate, only women do. Isn't Ngariba the one who started all this--dances, and the like, even though he was a man? The frog [#15] leads you to water [#16, a pond]. If you have your menstrual period and lack water, and you hear its "krrrr"--if you follow the sound, you will find water. Isn't the sun [#7] the guiding light of the Nyakanga? If something is wet, don't they have to put it out to dry?[9] The sun has many meanings. The meaning of the moon is this: when the moon arrives you know that you will menstruate since you are a woman. Doesn't the star [#6] reflect the moon's light? When it approaches it like this, you know your days are near. The basket [#19] represents that ritual when the beads are placed inside it; when an initiate [#14] is rewarded with money it's put in there. It protects everything. If there isn't a basket, you won't get anything. You're told, "You didn't bring a basket, you won't get anything today." Centipede [#18]: when it's there, won't it bite a child? It's bad. These [#3, lizard] only harm a child, the so-called gossips. The leader is this one [the snake, #9]. If you see it and follow it, you will find the way. If you see it going, trail along behind it. Where it sits is the tree at which you want to sit and not be seen by anyone. If it's not there like a guard, any person will come and watch what you are doing. But if it's there, they'll run away.

We got the dance *ngondo* [war] in the interior, far inland where the uncivilized people live.[10] My sister Momo Kikoi went there and saw it. When she was there she was invited in to watch. She liked it. It's a ritual. All that dance is just a ritual. She purchased it, but we don't sell it at all. Even if you cut our throats, we won't sell it. (We do sell *mbura*.) It's too dangerous. Somebody's daughter might fall into the pot of boiling water.

Ma Shea bought *mbura* from us, and we bought it from Pemba.[11] When Nyakanga received her initiates she received a mortar, an earthenware serving dish, a ladle. She got everything in *mbura*. That's when we started the secrets of *mbura*. The Pemba *makungwi* still dance *mbura*. They do it still, but clandestinely because since the Zanzibar revolution they have no strength, because they have no authority in town. Since our grandmothers' time long ago we were initiated into the dance. But those who came before us from Mozambique, those Makua on our side, they didn't have this *mbura* tree. Ma Shea's people didn't know its meaning. We

bought it by sending our mother there to Pemba. She bought
it and returned. If you buy that tree you will know the
meaning of the dance. The meaning of the mortar, the
meaning of bowing down comes with *mbura*.

The *msuku* tree is the same one I told you about,
mzongomzongo. Others have another one. They made it a
secret, because if someone discovered you, they could do you
harm, that is, if they knew about it. A person who doesn't
know about it will just think it's something we're doing.

Isn't *pembe* that silver chain?[12] It's four silver chains,
one kind of Nyakanga's jewelry. After Nyakanga has
"measured *pembe*" (that is, has done the dance), she wears
the chains.

Wedding Dances

First is the big drum dance; then the Stuffing Kapok
dance. Third is when the young girls her age do the things
for her. Isn't she the bride? So she is served until seven
days are up. And you, the *kungwi*, will wait and go and
check to see if she is clean [a virgin]. If she is unclean, then
there are problems. It's that same *vugo* dance of taking the
bride to the bath. The *Manyakanga* started it, and everyone
copied it. In the past my elders were taken to the bath that
same way. To perform *msondo* for her we danced that way.
The *kungwi* put the bride on her shoulders and went to the
bathroom. You returned with her celebrating and spent the
day at the house. *Bendera* [Red Sash Dance] is not very old.
It wasn't done at my wedding; it wasn't done for us. It was
worn at recent weddings. At my wedding *usufi* was just
beginning. At the start it wasn't as good as it is now. That
was the beginning of it. My *somo* brought pillowcases, and
we stuffed them and people danced. They didn't know how to
dance a thing. But now it's a real dance.

The present dance started a little while back, when the
makungwi argued with each other. Don't you see the dance
is different? This is different from Majengo's. We quarreled
over this *msondo* dance, the *makungwi*'s dance. We were all
together; everyone had her own rank. Then we came to
quarrel; they made fools of us. We gave them customary
gifts but they didn't reciprocate. We refused. We quarreled
long ago--Jabu had been born, and so had Halima and Rukia.
You know how it is. When people think they're smart they

don't get anything. We didn't want to fight, but they were
cheeky, they just wanted things for themselves. We didn't do
anything. We just did *usufi* ourselves, and then we started
bendera just to inflame the situation. They don't wear
sashes, or brassieres or dresses. We wore a complete outfit.
We didn't want to compete with them at all. We can't
compete with them, because all they know is what we know,
so how can one group have more strength? So we dance at
our place and they dance at theirs. We took Ma Shea with
us.

Lelemama

I danced after I had been divorced. But Halima's father
didn't want me to dance or to go outside. I was inside only,
cooking. He sent the servant out to buy everything and bring
it in the kitchen for me to cook. Lamini did not forbid me to
dance. I threw myself into it completely. If I wanted a
dress, he would take the material and sew. He would sew it
himself; he sewed for a living. He could sew anything you
wanted him to. My husband didn't stop me. For two or
three days he came and saw me and came back home. He
didn't ask questions. But Halima's father--you didn't dare
show your face outside. He would beat you until he got tired.
He was very strict.

I joined Banu Saada because of my sister's *kungwi*.[13]
She was our mother, our mother's friend, as if they were
sisters. I joined Banu Saada; I danced, my daughter danced
too after I had been divorced and Halima had given birth to
Rukia. Banu Saada was a real dance group, and we also
helped each other. A person would buy cloth; if money was
wanted, we would pay ten shillings. We slaughtered cows;
we went to the country. We really spent money dancing.
But we were number one; we knew the dance more than
anybody. We competed a lot with Ibinaa; we competed with
cows, trying to outdo one another in offering feasts. There
were brass bands, queens, all of that, but now it is finished.
We competed a lot with Ibinaa,[14] but we didn't fight. We
just wanted the dance. When we saw people wanting to
fight, we took off before it started. They danced inside; but
for competition they danced outside.

The people who started it--weren't they the women who
liked to do weddings? Their children brought *lelemama* from

Zanzibar. They said, "We'll dance it at our place." They
copied it here so that in Zanzibar it was nothing compared to
here. Arabs danced it, slaves danced it--they danced together
with their slaves. For the Arabs, the slaves were just to be
used.[15] The Arabs had their own weddings, but the slaves
had to serve them. Some women were slaves, but they
married freeborn men and had children by them. She has
both slave and free in her. If she wishes she follows the slave
way; if she doesn't, she follows the freeborn way.

Figure 1: Diagram of House Belonging to
Ma Shea, the Scene of the *Ngoma*

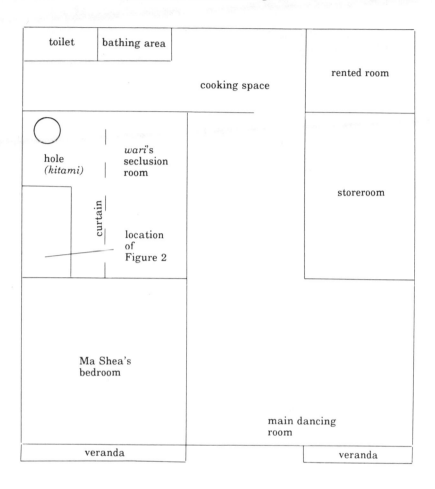

Figure 2: Floor Drawing

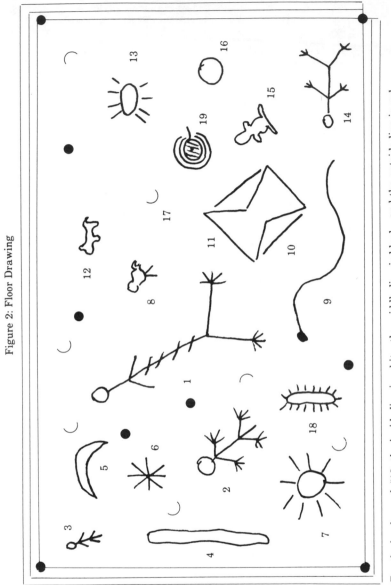

For the border and #19: the inside line is white, the middle line is black, and the outside line is red.

PART III

Shamsha Muhamad Muhashamy

Kaje wa Mwenye Matano and Zuena, 1973
Photograph by Margaret Strobel

Kaje wa Mwenye Matano, 1973
Photograph by Margaret Strobel

Introduction

Mwana Kutani, as Shamsa Muhamad Muhashamy is known to many people in Mombasa, is an energetic organizer for women and for members of the community as a whole. She is younger than Bi Kaje by nearly thirty years, and than Ma Mishi by nearly twenty. Yet age alone does not explain the difference in her outlook and activities. She had an unconventional upbringing as well.

In our interviews she had a clear idea of what she considered important to convey. Strobel was introduced to her as a leader of the women's community in Old Town by the Mazrui family, and our initial discussions surveyed women's issues. Subsequently Strobel returned and discussed two kinds of women's associations in which she had been active: *lelemama* dance associations and the Muslim Women's Institute, an organization that addresses social concerns of Swahili women. Thus by the time Strobel returned in 1975 and asked her for her life history, we had covered many topics. Unlike the other two, she ordered her presentation chronologically, in part because it was a summation of our hours of conversation. But perhaps the primary reason for her choosing this manner of presentation is that she had, by virtue of her class background, education, and experience, a sense of herself and her family as historical actors. (Bi Kaje conveyed this sense about some male ancestors, but not about herself.) Mwana Kutani had a greater self-consciousness in the sense of an awareness of the influences on her development as a person. She saw her family's history in terms of progress, and in her summation she attempts to evaluate that progress in the light of Western norms and influences.

Anyone of Shamsa Muhashamy's prominence is going to attract comment. Some people take her agitation for the Muslim Women's Institute and her presentation of her various efforts as self-aggrandizement and self-praise. Yet she has indeed worked hard, and in a manner unusual for Muslim women in Mombasa, to advance the interests of women and Swahili/Arab people generally.

At one point in the 1970s she was considering running for political office, but decided against it. In 1983 when Sarah Mirza visited her to confirm her agreement to publish the life history in this form, she was still vital and active in Mombasa affairs.

Shamsa Muhamad Muhashamy's strong sense of her ethnicity is rooted spatially in Mjua Kale, the neighborhood *(mtaa)* where her family has lived for nearly three hundred years. She identifies herself as Arab. Her father's side includes the Omani Arab lineages of Muhashamy and Mutwafi; her mother, the Hadrami Arab Shatry lineage. Her sense of neighborhood is so strong that she notes her mother is not from Mjua Kale, but rather from Kibokoni, an *mtaa* in the southern part of Old Town. (Mjua Kale also translates as "Old Town," hence the confusion in English.)

Although he was a good Muslim, Mwana Kutani's father raised her in an unorthodox manner. His attitude toward education is not unlike those of other male Muslim elites worldwide. Her family's conflicts over that upbringing make all the more immediate the real pain involved in the processes of social change. If her father appears to have been the primary influence in her childhood, her mother was a role model for the leadership skills she developed as an adult and put to effect in women's associations.

The *leso* boycott described here was Shamsa Muhashamy's first foray into organizing. In advocating that people refrain from buying large numbers of *leso*, Mwana Kutani and her mother were challenging a long-held custom among Swahili women. Photos from as early as the 1890s show coastal women wearing these colorful pairs of cloths. An observer reported as early as 1913 the fashion of changing designs monthly.[1] *Leso* or *kanga* (in Mombasa both terms are used)[2] are worn as clothing: older women like Bi

Kaje wear only *leso*, whereas young women around the home will wear Western dresses augmented by a *leso* around the waist. Beyond their use as clothing, *leso* are an important element in ritual exchanges at weddings, funerals, and the *makungwi's* rites.

In addition to the *leso* boycott, Mwana Kutani joined campaigns to curtail customary levels of spending on wedding and funeral celebrations. Such calls for restraint formed part of the news in the Arab weekly page of the *Mombasa Times* in the 1950s.[3] Although she cautions against merely rejecting one's own culture and adopting Western ways, and in fact criticizes the tendency toward a narrow nuclear family, she does not view expenditures on these celebrations as a mechanism for reinforcing extended kinship and friendship networks. Rather, she and other elite families view such ostentation as a waste of resources that ought to go toward education. They claim support for their views in Islamic norms that decry ostentation: for example, a wedding should be an occasion to feed the poor or give alms, but not to display one's wealth.

In observing the declining influence and fortunes of Arabs in colonial and independent Kenya, these elites view their own community's "backwardness" in such matters as part of the cause. Whether consciously or not, Mwana Kutani recognizes that through secular education people not only gain particular skills but also absorb Western values. This tension between adopting what is progressive in Western culture and retaining what is valuable of Swahili culture challenged the intellect and energies of Mombasa's reformers, from teachers like Sheik Al-Amin,[4] who criticized the sending of Muslim girls to Christian schools, to activists like Shamsa Muhashamy.

Mwana Kutani's movement through *lelemama* dance associations into the Muslim Women's Institute and politics reflects this process of sifting through one's own culture. In the end she rejected the expression of competition and factionalism, endemic to Swahili culture, that constituted much of what was exciting about *lelemama*.[5] Her account here stresses what she considers the foolish "hooliganism" of the groups.[6] But in other conversations she gave evidence of the training ground *lelemama* provided for the development of new skills.

My Early Life and Family

My Family

I am Shamsa Muhamad Muhashamy. I was born in 1919. Mombasa is our place, Old Town, Mjua Kale. This house was the house of Mwana Kutani, of Salim bu Khamisi Muhashamy. These houses are three together, and the neighborhood in the past was called Kutani. Indeed, by my well-known name I was called Mwana Kutani [child from within the stone wall]. I grew up in my father's and mother's house with my father's mother.[1] The whole family lived in this, our neighborhood; my father's mother and my mother's mother were together in this house because my mother was not a person of Old Town. She came from Mombasa, but she was one of the people of Kibokoni. For generations we have been the people of Mjua Kale. For generations we have been born only here in Mjua Kale. Our houses are the very ones of long ago; we still live in our grandfathers' homes. No one has built their own house. Where I live is my father's house that was my paternal grandfather's and my father's mother's--Mwana Ropa binti Muhamad Mutwafi. Her brother is Khamis Muhamad bin Jumaa, who is a special person here. People in Mombasa know that Muhamad bin Jumaa is the man who, when he died, was unmatched in wealth. His estate reached one lakh.[2] At that time one lakh was like forty million now. When the government counted his wealth it was one lakh. People were shocked. All the remaining children he had inherited that lakh. Each one was wealthy, including the renowned Khamis Muhamad, who became a famous wealthy man. Even that electric power

company is still his and his children's. So, I lived in our
home.

But as you know, the life I lived is different from my
playmates' lives here in our neighborhood and in Old Town.
This is because when my father was a child of about eighteen
he was sent by his parents to Egypt to study.[3] He studied
for a period of four years. Then unfortunately the uncle who
sent him died. There was no one else to send fees, so he was
brought back home. But the bit he gained was enough for
him and for us; it helped me and my four other brothers
progress. In observing life here and there, he saw great
differences. "I must open my child's ears," he felt. "In the
end that life will come here too. I want to help my children, I
must educate them, teach them, girls and boys. I should not
only teach the boys, but this girl too. If I were a rich person
I would send her to study in Europe or anywhere else." It
was still unknown for Arab children like us to be sent
anywhere. Not yet--and it came as a great shock. As far
back as I remember, my father had his work; he was a clerk
in the court. It was hard in those days to find a good person.
He was one who acted as a censor. If someone had a murder
case he was one who was called; that is, he was one of
Mombasa's intelligent men. He received a Mudirship[4] in
Mombasa. His area was the rural parts. This was before I
was born; when I was born he was already Mudir. Indeed he
was the first person to get a European-style job. As Mudir he
worked in the area of Kisauni and Bamburi up to Makirunge.

This is how I was born. They raised me well. And
when I reached the age to study I was put in religious
classes. I studied, but I attended these classes as a
youngster, before he enrolled me in school. Back then
children [girls] in our community were not to go out of doors
after age five or six. But my father took me to the farm, put
me on a bicycle, took me around without even a *buibui*. He
dressed me in hats. Everyone was shocked. "What's going
on, is she a European's child? Sometimes wearing hats.
Sometimes pants." And so I began to mature little by little.
Now other people said, "This is a European girl." Lots of
people said things like this. Why? Because my way of life,
my parents' way of raising me, wasn't the usual way.

My mother thought it was fine, and then later on she
felt even stronger that it was good. When her husband died,
she saw how I was getting on when left on my own. I had

my brothers, but each one had his own affairs. I recall my
mother did not live like other people's mothers. That is, she
was driven about in my father's car. He had a car very
early. I remember him teaching my mother how to drive.
And he taught her to ride a bicycle even before me. He
played tennis; he made a court on the farm and bought
rackets. Because of these things everyone said this man
Muhamad bin Salim has a mind of his own. Why do things
this way? He didn't shut his wife off like the wives of his kin
who veiled themselves and were kept inside. If a European
friend or an Asian came by, he would call his wife to join the
conversation. To do so in our society was an impossibility. It
was absolutely impossible at that time to have your wife be
visible to a stranger. Even for a child of eight or nine, one
could not bring her out into the street or bring her to the
house of a man; even a woman who was an outsider couldn't
see her. But in my case things were not like that. In
Kisauni my father looked after his mother's, Mwana Ropa's,
farms. We went there during the week to stay. He had
married a European wife, but she converted.[5] Later he
divorced her, after we had all been born except for my
youngest brother. He was married to her for about eight
years. But he stayed with my mother until he died; he died
before my mother.

    She didn't live like others in our community. She went
another way. So my father could bring her out in public, in
places full of men, and have her be part of dance associations.
He went to local farms, and dances would be performed.
Wasn't he a Mudir? If a person was a Mudir or Liwali and if
you went out with your wife, you had to mingle with people,
give speeches; and my mother would sit with him. This was
a big surprise. People were upset, especially my maternal
grandfather's kin. They said, "Our child has been ruined."
She was a Shatry. They felt what he was doing was not
correct. But, what good was it to protest? He was the
husband, and a husband has the right to do what he wishes
with his wife.[6]

    So I got a double dose of it because my mother was the
daughter of respectable people, but I was my father's child.
Of course he would raise me as he wished. He dressed me in
pants. People made a lot of noise when he took me around
with my face bare. I didn't put on a *buibui* early, not until
near puberty. Then I was dressed in a *buibui*.[7] I didn't run

from people. I wasn't afraid because I lived at home, that is, I lived far away from the relatives who objected.

Education

When I reached the age of nine, I was enrolled in school because I was old enough. I was sent to the Buxton School, CMS [Church Missionary Society].[8] The teacher at that time was Miss Lloyds, but no English was taught; it was not yet allowed. My father was not pleased because even he himself could teach me Swahili at home. After two years he withdrew me from that school. He took me to the Asian school, but they refused me because I didn't know their language. He tried to look for a European school for me, but it was impossible; education back then was difficult to come by. My brothers studied at the Arab [Boys'] School. Many boys received education. The problem was for me, a girl. I could not enter European school because of discrimination. There were Indian and Goan schools, but they didn't want people of other tribes, because their schools were privately run by their associations.[9] The CMS didn't teach English, and when my father spoke to them and asked them to teach me just a little at a time, they said, "No, the government doesn't give us permission to teach girls." You know, those missionaries can only follow orders.

And these people (my relatives) completely opposed the missionaries. My mother's paternal grandfather came from Arabia; those were the Shatrys. They wondered, "Why is he allowing our child to attend missionary school? She will go and sin, because she'll change her religion." Now, I found a girl whose father thought, "What Muhamad bin Salim did is right, and I will put my child in school too." And so the two of us went to school. But this didn't last, because I returned home and studied there, but my companion quit her studies. She didn't care for it. So, with my father's persistence and their hassling, I only studied for one year. If it wasn't for that I would even have gone to Europe. My mother's relatives, her father, completely refused and said, "You must remove her."[10] But I was thankful to my father because he wanted me to be smarter than the men. Every day he said, "If I let her be stupid, these men will oppress her."

My First Husband

My father died while I was still young, before I was
married. I was near puberty. But he was able to accept the
proposal money. When my proposal came he received it
himself, because he did not want me to follow customs where
you hide yourself and where women don't see other women
and don't see men. This was impossible because of the way I
was brought up. We went hunting, and he gave me a gun.
He took me to the beach, taught me to fire a rifle, taught me
to drive, and gave me a bicycle to ride. He looked for a
husband for me who he knew was sophisticated. Because he
had lived with him, he knew he was someone who was
educated and was a customs clerk. In fact the man who
married me was the first Arab officer to be "second grade."[11]
So we lived happily, and this man agreed to my continuing
the same lifestyle. There were many people who brought
proposals, but my father looked for a man who wasn't rich,
who was poor, but who had his own work. He said, "I cannot
take my child and put her in an uncomfortable relationship
because of money. She might be treated badly."

Manyanya was my *somo*,[12] who took me to my husband
on our wedding day. When you reach puberty, she's the one
who explains things to you. By our custom we did not hold
dances or do anything special. People said these things were
for slaves, for lower-class people. But now even people of
freeborn ancestry do it. She's the one who takes you to your
husband, explains things--you should respect him, he's your
husband. And since at the beginning you do not know how to
speak to him, you do not yet know to greet him with respect.
That's how she became my *somo*.

After my father's death I had to marry, so I married
and left home and went to live in Funzi. This was the
beginning of my adult life. Muhamad Khamis Shakhsi was
my husband. He worked for the Customs Office. His father
was friends with a European, so he gave him his child and
said, "Teach him for me." He was educated by his father's
friend--the District Commissioner, I think.

I didn't live long in Funzi. I only stayed there two
years. But I lived a happy life without thinking about
weddings, about funerals, I only thought about married
life.[13] Then we were transferred to Malindi; in 1934 I went
to Malindi.

We returned to Mombasa in 1942. Then our life started going bad. My husband began to change. His mind changed from drinking. If a person lives in an out-station and then here, it's a big problem. There he is on his own; here he has supervisors.

In 1946 and 1947 we had settled down and lived a home life, traveling to Zanzibar and Dar es Salaam to rest. My husband hadn't divorced me, but we lived apart. After he came back in '46 and '47 is when I forced him to divorce me. I sued him and took him to court. I wasn't happy, I wanted him to divorce me so that I could find another husband to marry me. He was giving me trouble, and to me he wasn't a husband anymore. In 1948 I tried hard until in '49 he divorced me at the Kadhi's.[14] In '50 I was very ill. It was a ruptured appendix. I had an operation and was ill for many days.

My Second Husband

In '52 I found somebody else who wanted to marry me.[15] His name was Ali Salim Jeneby. He was a relative. He used to work for Kelly. He was a law clerk. He is one of the people who went to Addis Ababa during the war. He married an Arab lady and had children. When he came back, he had a wife and children. Now, we came to an agreement. We talked, and he said he would marry me. I said it was better for me to leave that life of hooliganism[16] and find a husband to marry me and live. He married me in 1953.

I knew him before we married. A long time ago he used to come to our place, but I didn't flirt with him. He went to my friend and told her, "Call your friend, I want to marry her." I talked to him about some troublesome things, and he told me, "Quit your hooliganism." I told him, "Even I don't want to engage in hooliganism. But I am used to being with people. You must give me permission to go out sometimes, because I cannot be closed in a lot. I've been free for many days." If a man confines somebody who has been free for a long time, there will necessarily be problems. He agreed and said, "I cannot lock you up." He was as old as I. My first husband was much older, but my second husband was smarter than that one. I announced my conditions. This man was well known here. He had many problems, problems to do with politics. He even quarreled with [Liwali] Mbarak

bin Ali Hinawiy because of scholarships for their brothers and
sisters, a matter that involved people in government. You
know in those days it was like saying that people were eating
government money by themselves, and they were giving
scholarships only to each other. So he didn't care about
government people here, because they did the opposite of
government policies. He had some education, so he wanted to
investigate matters properly. People should get their rights,
according to him.

My brothers and other people told me, "You cannot
handle this. Don't let him marry you. You will have
problems and later regret it. He shouldn't marry you." I
thought, "Now I'm grown up, and to go around like this is
stupid. As a human being changes, their thinking changes
too. I have enjoyed myself and done this and that with my
friends. I need to realize that people should be able to come
to me and my brothers, and the children too need me. To be
a complete person, I should find a husband to marry me. If I
don't do him wrong, how can he do me wrong?" People gave
me an example, they said, "You see he has a wife that he
really mistreats. He brought his wife from a faraway place."
I insisted if something is meant to be it will be. There are
things that if we want to remove we can do so, but things
that God wants we cannot remove. If God wants, He can
block your ears and blind your eyes. To block my ears means
that people will tell me things and I will not listen. Many
people tried to stop me and friends said, "You do not know
this man. This man is a liar." He did a lot of good to me,
and every time we met he said good things to me. I looked at
him and saw him as someone I could not do any evil to. I
would be under him and listen to him. Why would he do
wrong to me? I must listen to him, I have agreed to put
myself in a hole. Isn't that so? Even my mother wasn't
happy, but she said, "You are a grown person, and you know
I am behind you." Also I was feeling uneasy because there
were people I couldn't avoid until I was married.[17] If I
would get married everybody will mind their own business
and go. I got married and we lived here with my husband.
We lived here at my place because I said, "I can't follow you
because I have my mother and she is old." He agreed to live
here. We lived here in '54 and '55, now we started to
arrange things for the Muslim [Women's] Institute--the Arab
Women['s] Association.

82037

Children

I did not give birth to even a single child. Because I didn't have any children, I took those children. Their mother left here pregnant, and I was sick. She went to deliver, but the child died and so did the mother. So now these two children were left; Muhamad Said was two years old, and Khuleta was one. So these children Muhamad--have stayed with me up to now.

LINCOLN CHRISTIAN COLLEGE AND SEMINARY

My Work in Women's
Organizations

The *Leso* Boycott

I watched my mother creating all kinds of organizations.
One time we did an organization for *leso*.[1] At that time,
1942-1943, people were making a lot of noise. It was like
this. These Indians brought tickets for reserving *leso*. Those
tickets had conditions which said that this ticket expires in
seven or eight days, and if you haven't bought your *leso*, you
will forfeit your money. I read those conditions and I
understood them. You'll buy *leso* for eight shillings, and the
reservation costs one shilling. Now somebody, poor thing,
would give out one shilling quickly to reserve a *leso*, and that
was their trick. Today, the third of the month, they will
come up with a good sample, and then the fifth of the month
they will come out with a better sample. Then I will think,
"Oh, this is a better sample than the other one," so I will give
another shilling to hold this one. Now I will have two tickets.
When it comes to the fifteenth of the month, they will come
up with a sample that is even better than the other two.
They have all the samples before, but on purpose they show
the bad ones first so that those are sold out, and then they
take out the good ones. So I will buy another ticket, that is,
now I will have three tickets. And all these *leso* will be sold
at the end of the month. Now I have three tickets worth
three shillings. When the end of the month comes around I
will not buy all three, I will buy one or two *leso*. If I buy one
leso, the other one or two shillings will go to the Indians.
This two shillings will not only be left by one person, but by
many people all over Mombasa. How much money goes for

nothing? And nobody sees that money again.

So now I made an effort and went to every house and collected the tickets. You will find in some poor person's house one hundred shillings worth of unredeemed tickets. I went around in a car with a loudspeaker telling people that we have opened an office to defend ourselves against the Indians. We told people to bring all their tickets. So, many tickets were brought. There were over 100,000 when we counted them. You see the way the Indians exploited us. And these people didn't understand, because they didn't have any education. We called a meeting and many people came. From Majengo and the rural areas, they all came. I told them that this was exploitation. These *kanga* were only worn by Muslim women from Mombasa, Tanga, Dar es Salaam, Msambweni, Malindi, Vanga, and so on. I told them, let's not buy *kanga*, and let's see who will buy them now. Let's not reserve any *kanga*. If anyone wants to buy *kanga*, they should buy them without reserving them first, because we have given the Indians a lot of money from the deposits. Every day the Indians were raising the prices of *kanga*.

We told people we will try to order *leso* from Europe. At that time Japan and Britain were exporting cloths.[2] If you sent a design, they would send you the cloths. But our people thought that this was a very easy thing, that is, to import cloths. These Indians had built up their business over a long time. They had already started doing application forms, they'd been accepted to make samples, and to send them--the entire process of ordering. It took many days. You can't just do that kind of thing and send a deposit. It requires a lot of money. At that time one crate was about 6,000-8,000 shillings for one kind of *leso*, because in one crate there were many sets of *kanga*. You can send that to Dar es Salaam, Malindi, everywhere, just that one kind. So the least you would need to order is 6,000 shillings per crate. At that time, one set of *leso* cost between 12 and 15 shillings. So how can we do that at one time? For me, I couldn't front that much money. It required those business people who are used to it. Now the Indians were worried. People stopped buying *leso*. We started looking for cloths in Tanganyika. They were sent to us from Tanganyika. Now, our people didn't understand that getting anything in this world entails problems. People must face problems at first. Independence does not come without hardship. We won't get good cloths, but it's OK,

we'll just wear what we have until later, when things will
improve. When these people saw that we were only giving
them one kind at a time, they wanted five or six kinds.
Where would we find money like that? And the basis of all
this is their lack of education. This saddened me.

This continued for many days; for about one year they
didn't buy *leso* from the Indians. We brought a few *leso* from
Tanganyika. The Indians came in full force and said, "Stop
this game. We will give you money so we can sell clothes."
They took a big loss. But what really spoiled it was that
people went back to buy clothes from these Indians. We felt
really sorry, because they didn't have enough sense. They
didn't know that when people fight there has to be difficulty.
This was our war with the Indians. If we had continued, we
would have had our own shop.

Since 1943 I have tried to open the eyes of women in
my community and explain to them. But they refused to see
what was correct. This really saddened me. We incurred
many losses, more than 8,000 shillings, because when we
gave other people *leso* to sell, they did not return the money.
They went back to buy clothes from the Indians, and the
Indians grew more bitter and sold their clothes at an even
more expensive price. Now one set of *leso* is 50 shillings.
But if at that time we had had faith in each other and had
been more patient, we would have been at a good place now.
They couldn't be patient. They wanted new clothes every
day. Then there were even more problems.

Cloths completely disappeared. The government stopped
them being ordered because of fights. They broke unity and
bought *leso* secretly. At that time, if a woman was seen
standing at a shop and buying clothes, she was beaten.
There was a woman who was beaten, and we all were taken
to the police station. Right then I called a meeting and we
collected 2 shillings from each person. We got 12,000
shillings for bail for the woman who was arrested.

At that time I realized that I had a voice, and I tried,
even though I didn't succeed; I have become a leader. I tried
to open their ears. There are people up to now who don't put
a deposit on *leso*. That practice has faded. I broke it
completely. For the question of deposit, I won. As for the
buying of *leso,* I didn't win. The practice of deposits had
completely faded, but now it's starting to come back again
because of the younger generation who were not part of the

fight. That was the first thing I did in my life, and everyone knew about it. It wasn't something I did to show myself off, but rather to help the community see that we are being exploited and that we are at the bottom. Why should we be oppressed and made fools of? So that's what I did in my house and in my courtyard, and I was listened to.

Whenever we were together, I tried to explain to them that we cannot leave the customs and beliefs of our grandfathers. But there are other things that are foolish. At the same time, we cannot just follow the Europeans. We will only follow what we think is good; the bad we will not follow. Everyone imitates the good practices of others. Our ancestors had big weddings and funerals, but they had nothing to do and the cost of living was low. It used to be that people would bring things to the house and cook and eat, and that was enough. But now you have to buy everything. Today, every time we meet with people we tell them, "Leave this business of big funerals and weddings, and let's cut down." If we continue with this, we will not progress. Today if someone has a wedding, they must spend 25,000-30,000 shillings.[3]

Lelemama

In 1945-46 my mother and father belonged to Banu Saada. A group is fun, it's enjoyable. During their time I didn't have my own say about things. After my father died, only my mother was left, and Banu Saada seemed to be fading. So I looked for a strong group to join. That's not all-- my father was dead, and my mother was too old and didn't participate anymore. She was there in name only. On the other side there was my group of friends and my cousins, so I had to join Ibinaa.[4] In our area there was nobody who was in Banu Saada, it was my father alone, like a family group. Everybody was surprised that my father was in that group; it was only because it was his brother's group. We didn't enter Ibinaa for any special reason, we just inherited it. But then conflicts arose.

All this time we had heard that people used to fight and used to slander each other in song. But we only heard about this. Later we ourselves, young women, saw people fighting and cutting each other's ears. At that time the government was in our hands. My brother was in the police, my uncle

was in court, that's how it was. We who were dancing were
like siblings. Even when we had a riot, it wasn't much. We
were young then, with young blood. So I participated in the
dance and really regretted it later on, because I was a real
hooligan. The leaders were people like Bi Imu, but they were
old. So we had to compete with Banu Saada until we ended
this business of competition and cooled off. Then little rumors
started: Banu Saada is like this, Ibinaa is like this. Then
they started talking behind our backs, saying that the people
who were clever were Banu Saada. So we started competing.
I danced so much I didn't even eat my food properly. My
biggest desire was to win, to put an end to this hassle.
People competed with cows.

We first gave them five cows for a feast. They took
these and then gave us back ten cows. We gave them fifteen
cows. They did not come to get them. We defeated them by
that amount. Then they said, "Give us our five cows." So
we had beaten them. We competed with them for over a
year. We danced, and I was the one involved in the
paperwork and the distribution of the papers. So I went and
did up the statements and advertisement that we had won
and put them in the cars. We had about one thousand cars.
The whole of Mombasa was looking at us. We were wearing
skirts and blouses like the Royal Air Force. We came down
with drums like the European air force. Now my life was
completely spoiled because of dancing, like this, because I had
danced nearly naked. [That is, without a *buibui*.] But it was
our intention to win. I did not dance on the platform, I was
the advisor and propaganda person. But everyone else
danced. Nobody was left out, especially at the time of the
fight. It was a must for everyone to come out so that we
could win. It was victory!

These dances used to be danced inside. Freeborn women
used to dance inside. They put up a cloth fence and posted
guards; men didn't come inside. But these competition dances
removed all modesty. We came out naked because we came
out into the open without a fence, and the men were looking
at us. The grownups were very upset by it. They said that
these children have been spoiled. Like me, I had my uncle at
the time of the competition, but I wouldn't go to see him
because I was scared he would scold me. I had my aunts and
grandmothers, but I was scared to see them because we knew
we were damaging our respectability. We competed on the

streets here in Bondeni at Bwana Kombo's. The men gathered around us like a fence. This was the first time that Mombasa women came out and danced openly. We came down from Changamwe with guns and uniforms like the Royal Air Force without caring about anything. We saw people, but we pretended we did not see them. Because we wanted victory, we broke the rules. We came out dancing without veils. And the men, our brothers and our husbands, all came and watched us. We thought, "We have broken our parents' orders, we might as well win this." The women themselves wanted to come out. They were so ready that even when their husbands stopped them, they said, "It doesn't matter, you may divorce me. I'll go and compete."

We did this just for the competition, not for our independence. We did this, and then we went back to our normal lives, but we had lost our shame because people who were in seclusion were different from people who went outside. After the competition we went back to our normal lives; but we had gained something. It strengthened other people who could now go out without veils the way they did on that day.[5]

Then only the demise of the dances remained. The government finally stopped them. I was able at the dance to fight with two hundred or one hundred and fifty people, and I came out unhurt. Other people had cuts and had to be sent to the hospital because of the fight. The older people tried hard so that it shouldn't get to the elders in the government. They tried to call us and stop us. If it had happened now, we wouldn't have been able to create this chaos because the government is solid. But at that time, the government was ours. Nowadays the police would have come and got me, but then not even once did I go to the police. Others had to have stitches, and we did not want to have a court case. We were just naughty. We liked to fight, so we couldn't go and make a report to the police, and the others didn't either. People in the city tried to stop the chaos, and the elders were ashamed. They tried to get the government to call us and stop our permit for dancing. So, our permit was stopped and we were refused the right to dance. What was left was fighting, and then we stopped fighting and made peace. We hated each other for a long time, but then we united. I regretted it very much because life was so short, and what I had done wasn't good. I realized that it was childish and stupid for people to be fighting. We are so few people, and then we fight.

I started a *lelemama* organization called Combine, so that we could get everyone together to help one another. The women who danced in Combine were not the ones in Banu Saada or Ibinaa, because it was the young generation, we youngsters. We were just kids; grownups were in Banu Saada. I was in Ibinaa because it was part of our family. It wasn't our club, it was that of our mothers and grandmothers. But this Combine was a group that I formed myself.

At that time I started having a social life. I had had my domestic life, and now I came out to join the life of the community, to know the state of other people's lives. I joined associations. I called everyone together and we made an agreement, because one person alone cannot be a founder, she must think and then call her comrades.

We agreed to form a group. I gave it the name Combine, so that despite the war between Ibinaa and Banu Saada we would unite and become one, so that we could start new things. In the past there was Banu Saada and Ibinaa, there was no president, or treasurer, or vice-treasurer. We made a rule that if someone was bereaved, we would give her fifty shillings, or if she had a wedding she would put out a tray and we would give her fifty shillings as a group to help her. It went on for many days, for years--five or six years. The purpose, to my mind, was to bring everyone together in one place to dispel that strife. But we were not ready. People don't have the political judgment and good sense, so it wasn't possible, and the club was destroyed.

Muslim Women's Institute

That's when I formed the Muslim Women's Institute.[6] Let's take people from Banu Saada and Ibinaa and put them together again. Now we started to want to be like human beings again. The Muslim Women's Institute was founded in 1957. My husband Ali Salim Jeneby arranged it all by himself. He was a man of politics as I have told you. Now a committee had to be formed. We lost a lot of money. In Banu Saada and Ibinaa we spent thousands and thousands in weekend picnics. We spent two to three thousand for nothing. During the war this was a lot of money. Other men gave money without thinking. I told my husband, "Give a cow," and he did. Five to six people at a time gave cassava, rice, *biriani*,[7] and bands and everything for the weekend, a lot of money was lost.

I came to think that if we had collected the money, we could have made a name for ourselves. Now my brain is working like a person's brain should. We are very backward. The way we have problems, why don't we form our institute and have our own name and be able to appear at social functions like the Indians? The Indians have two hands, and we have two hands too. We must unite and be like them: we are behind. We are not united, we are beaten by the police on the roads when there is a function and we want to see someone. We must form an association, so that it is known that we have our association and our savings. And for our children we should have a place to educate them, and we should progress the way people progress. Other people said, "Let's join with the Indians." But I said, "No, we'll have our own; we will not join the Indians. Here the Indians are foreigners, with us it's the lack of education that's making us backward. We would have had a social hall a long time ago. How was it that the Goans had their own association, how come the Indians had halls and services and a school? We've been here, born here, all the wealth is ours, all the buildings are ours, the plots of land are ours. Why didn't we have a social hall?[8] All this was due to lack of education.

So my husband said to me, "Wait, I'll show you how to do this. Invite about forty people and explain to them and then form your own committee." "How many people are in a committee?" He said, "Secretary,[9] let's do the application and registration." This was the first time a woman's organization was registered through Nairobi--the Muslim Women's Association. Many of the associations were for fun. They couldn't make any requests. That's how we did it. He was the one who helped me and did everything. There was just a secretary by name. He was the one that typed, did the application, and wrote letters and everything else. He had all the papers. My education advanced then. We were able to start a club and arrange files. The files have remained at my place up to now. We continued on very well. The problem was that he didn't like somebody to go out and roam around. He didn't like a person to make friends, and I'm used to that. Many times I couldn't go to a wedding, but that was OK. I agreed to it. But he agreed that I could form an organization at Bi Itidali's, Said Seif's wife.

The association was formed, and it was called the Arab Women['s] Institute.[10] We came to have some say. I was elected treasurer. They trusted me to keep the money. Up till today when people are elected, they don't want to take me away from that position. He helped me a lot in my life and I was happy. He helped me with the club so that we were able to get anything we wanted. Even when we made petitions to go and beg for votes, he was in it too. We lived well together. I have explained to you how at first I was just the head of an association, and the second time I was elected by the people themselves. They elected me. (I did not elect myself the second time in Combination [Combine].) They elected me the head, so I became secretary under Fatuma Muhamadi. The third time I was treasurer. Since that time in '57 until today I am treasurer of the Muslim Women's Institute.

Politics

After forming the association in '57 and '58 and '59 we formed another club, a political one. The men formed a political club, and they said, "How can we get the women? Who will draw the women? And who among the men will stand up and do that?" At that time it was a problem here to stand for office. I don't think it was possible to find a woman who would say that she would stand. It was hard to find someone. If you did, then her husband or uncle would refuse--because there were a lot of men during the time of Mwambao. There wasn't a scarcity of men, but there were only a few women; and then our women were not able to face such meetings. This is what made the women of the Muslim Institute go to the Oceanic Hotel. Many women hadn't been to the Oceanic. Before independence it was hard for someone who wasn't up-to-date to enter a big hotel. No one was allowed except the colonialists, who were the ones who gave people permission to enter. But because of the association they gave permission. So we rented the hotel to make those people happy. Those men thought, "Let's look for Shamsa binti Muhashamy, Mwana Kutani as she is known. Maybe she will stand up and help us."[11]

Now we come to the political time of my life. I was married then and my husband loved politics. And because we would be together, he did not oppose me even once for something to do with politics. The people that he associated with were the ones that always quarreled with the government. This party was called the Coast People's Party, the party of the coast. People came and talked to me, including Freiya, Mbarak Ali's daughter, Swafiya Salim Muhashamy, and Salwa. They had done their Cambridge exams.[12] They were at an age where they could do anything. So Freiya came, she found herself alone, and she was young. She was capable of doing anything but she was alone. She and the founder of the club came. They wanted all the ideas, so they came to me and said, "We want to talk with you. We want you to join hands with us so that you can be in this club with us." But I said, "I have tried a lot here in Mombasa but nothing came of it. It's better if you join up with another club because here nobody understands what we're doing. When people want to progress, they fall back. Here the thing that kills them is bigheadedness and jealousy, they think, 'How can this person progress?' So when they see why someone has progressed they'll try to destroy that. We must give birth to four or five generations before people understand how to express their humanity fully." So they said, "It's all right, we will try. 'You have to get lost to know the way.' We will find out from our speeches, and you will stand up and talk. So if they follow we will all be saved, if they leave us we will all be defeated." Men from here, well-known people, came and agreed with them. There came Bwana Ali Shikeli, Bwana Khamis Kilungu, and him, Ali Salim Jeneby, and Mwalim Rashid Baakuli, who was the president. Several people joined, all from the coast. We had a complete party.

Here too I was confronted with a difficult life. Here there was KADU and KANU and we added our coast party, the Coast People's Party.[13] Our friends had good sense. They formed only two parties, KADU and KANU. We formed ours, CPP, that is, including Malindi and Lamu up to Mogadishu and down to Vanga. When we opened our eyes there were here at the coast about thirty parties competing with CPP. KADU and KANU were just the same. So our tribe has formed about thirty parties. Now the majority had formed one party and we the minority had formed eleven, how can that be? But we stood up without fear. The KADU people thought that we were spoiling it for them because they wanted us to join them to defeat KANU; others thought we

should join KANU and beat KADU. But we went from here
to there, and we were right in the middle. If we had united
we would have gotten at least two or three seats. But we
didn't unite; we had many parties.

I am a famous person in Mombasa. If you ask someone,
"Who is that woman who used to speak on the microphone
during CPP?" they will say, "I know her very well." I have
helped Mombasa people throughout my life. From the age of
twenty-two until now I have been with the people. That
place Mwembe Tanganyika used to be filled with people, men
and women, young and old, and I used to stand on the table
with my microphone, and the police were there and all the
people. I used to preach to people about my politics until it
got into their ears. There wasn't a Mombasa man who could
interfere with me. I wasn't scared of a club or a spear or
anything at all.

People didn't like us. They thought we were spoiling
things. I stood until the week of the election, until the day of
counting, until I knew we had lost. We were bound to lose.
But we have the right to be here. The date on our door is
275 years ago, the date of our house. My father remembers
seeing it. Without a doubt this is my home. But we made a
mistake because of our misdeeds and our stupidity, and we
did not think ahead.

But people have seen what has come. Now they have
seen many changes. We thank our leader [Jomo Kenyatta],
he has given us justice. It's better to have education, and our
rights haven't been stolen from us. We have them. The
person who owns a house hasn't had it taken away. And we
live in peace. We've received other rights that we didn't have
under colonialism, that was the peak of my politics. I was
chosen, I moved quickly until we finished. Now we are
progressing. Now what is left is to choose the town
counselors.

Now Mwana is right there involved in real politics. No
one in Mombasa can stand for election unless they come to
me. It's absolutely necessary. What they fear is, "If we
don't check with her, we will not get a majority of the
women." I thank the women from my part of Old Town and
the others too. It's clear that they listen to me and they like
me as their leader. Because if they didn't like me, they
wouldn't keep choosing me. It's not only the women of
Mombasa, but all the women in general. Recently I was

chosen in 1972 in Tononoka by the African women and our women to become the vice-chairman of Maendeleo ya Wanawake[14] here at the coast. So I returned and I became a member of KANU. I now was chosen in KANU. I was chosen in the Kuze branch as vice-chairman of KANU for Old Town. Sharif Nassir was chairman. I'm not saying that I'm very clever, and I don't choose myself. I'm chosen by the people. If they didn't see that I was someone worth choosing, they wouldn't have chosen me.

They saw I was someone who worked. I still hold these positions. I'm in the Serani School Parents Association. It's customary to have a committee for adults to see how the children are doing. Whenever the committee is called at Serani to see how the children can be helped and what the mothers need to be told about, I'm one of the people who look after the welfare of the children. I'm one of the people on the Old Town committee who are able to visit hospitals and see how the sick are cared for. I have written two letters to Pandya Hospital when I found the sick were complaining. Thank God our requests have been granted in that they now get good food and clothing. Once the government stopped giving children scholarships. This was before Mzee Kenyatta gave permission for Standards I-IV[15] to be free. It was hard for our children. We were poor. If somebody had four or five children, it was hard to pay their fees. So they used to get scholarships to help them. Suddenly the government stopped that. We tried very hard. We sent applications requesting help for people.

Reflections

I have helped many people, and I have sacrificed for politics. But now I'm old, my duty to politics must be put aside. I feel that now I should just work on social issues because we do not understand, and I have seen that people do not understand the benefits of a woman going into politics. I wanted to make a big effort to fight for our women, especially because this is International Women's Year,[16] so that there is a woman from our community joining the council, so that we wouldn't be told we didn't accomplish anything for the year of the women. If any other woman would have asked me to give her the position, I would gladly have supported her. It would be better than giving it to a man, because I

have seen that many men run for office for the sake of
competition. Those men are people we fight for all the time.
Without women, they cannot be. We give many votes to
men, but they just run for competition. They wanted us to
help them, because when I stand for office I don't stand just
for women. I stand for both women and men all the time. If
something comes up, it happens to both women and men.

I'm a person who has quarreled a lot, and I have
competed for many days. First it was for the dance. Second,
I competed in politics. I have formed the club of the Muslim
Women's Association [Institute]. The other women of my
community, instead of joining, formed their own in
competition.[17] I didn't agree, and until today I have my own
club. But now I see it's not necessary to compete.

I have served the community from age twenty-two until
now. Whoever comes and says they want to go to the D.C.
[District Commissioner], I take them. Whoever says they
want a passport, I do it for them. Whoever wants a birth
certificate, I do it for them. Whoever says they want help for
their children to go to school, they will attend. Whoever says
somebody is sick and wants to go to the hospital, they go. If
she comes to my door, she will not be turned away. I have
made a great effort to send more than twenty-four children
out of the country for further studies. It's the club, but it's
my effort. Who formed the club? We sent girls as well as
boys. Even though girls need more help, there are very few
who have good [examination] results. So should we leave
those scholarships to go to waste? To get something is to get
something. We give even more scholarships than before to
girls. I tried hard. Where my community is concerned, I do
not rest. But now I've reached the point where I've left
politics.

The good old days are over. These days, because of the
way life is, everyone is hectic, a person can't take time for
someone else. Like the Europeans, a person only knows her
family. It used to be that my grandmother or her sister
would come and take me and we would spend the day
together. But now it's just the nuclear family. I think they
acted that way in the past because they hadn't become
"modern." When you become modern, you lose your
sensitivity. This European sophistication brings the feeling
that you and your family alone are enough. In the past you
had to know everybody in the family; everyone was your

sibling. We had our religion and our own ways; they were at peace inside. This is no longer the case. I don't know if this is because people didn't have work, or because it was our way of life. I don't think sophistication misleads one. Education is progressive. It teaches cleverness. You see that it is not necessary to go and visit someone all the time, you have your own work. This has brought about more economic activity, because in the old days women did not have any work except to make mats and do housework.[18]

APPENDIX

Swahili Language

Swahili is spoken by thirty million people in eastern Africa,[1] mainly in Kenya, Tanzania, and Uganda, with smaller numbers in eastern Zaire, southern Somalia, Rwanda, Burundi, Mozambique, Malawi, and Zambia. Perhaps twenty million of these have learned it as a second language.[2] Its diffusion throughout east Africa reflects historic processes.

Although precise historical reconstruction of the early development is difficult, Swahili is thought by some scholars to have differentiated from related languages in the ninth century A.D.[3] Prior to that time, horticulturalist speakers of proto-Bantu began spreading from the area of eastern Nigeria east and south in the second millennium B.C., displacing hunting and gathering populations who spoke Khoisan languages and meeting, in eastern Africa, Cushitic speakers who were farmers and pastoralists.[4] By the second century A.D., proto-Northeastern Coastal Bantu speakers (NECB is a subgroup of Eastern Bantu. in turn a subgroup of the Bantu language group) was probably spoken in the area to the west and south of Mombasa. As population dispersed from there, proto-Sabaki speakers moved north to the Juba-Tana area of southern Somalia and northern Kenya, resulting in communities of iron-working subsistence farmers and fishers there by 500 A.D.[5] By 800 A.D. an early form of Swahili was spoken as far south as Kilwa in southern Tanzania. The differentiation between northern and southern Swahili dialects developed early, in the ninth century, and Mombasa's dialect Kimvita separated relatively early, with the town being founded ca. 1000 A.D.

Swahili communities along the coast existed as small villages, with houses made of irregular coral blocks as well as mud and wattle. After the ninth century Swahili settlements shifted from a land-based to a sea-based economy, a change marked by residents' move onto adjacent islands along the coast. Thus the early history of Mombasa involved Mombasa Island; the concentration of population on the nearby mainland has resulted from the rapid population growth of the colonial period.

From its origins in the ninth century until the eighteenth century, Swahili remained a coastal language, spanning Somalia, Kenya, Tanzania, and Mozambique. With the arrival of the Portuguese in the sixteenth century and the subsequent rise of the Omani Arab political and economic power in east Africa came the historical forces that spread Swahili inland from these coastal communities as a language of trade. Swahili moved to inland Tanzania as the lingua franca of the slave traders; Zanzibari-based traders did not similarly penetrate Kenya.

The slave trade and European economic expansion drew missionaries, who played a major role in the transliteration of Swahili into roman script (it was previously written only in Arabic script), the recording of early texts, and the preparation of dictionaries. Two of these, Frederick Johnson's *A Standard Swahili-English Dictionary*[6] and Ludwig Krapf's *A Dictionary of the Suahili Language*,[7] are still major sources of information, the former used more widely by Swahili language students.[8]

Similarly, colonial rule expanded the use of Swahili because of the need to integrate a much larger territory under a single political structure. Particularly in Tanganyika, it came to be used as the language of administration.[9] As a consequence of these various factors, Swahili was more widely spoken in Tanganyika than in Kenya in the colonial period. This pattern has been changed, however, by the media and the introduction of Swahili into the curriculum with the expansion of education in post-colonial Kenya.

Kimvita Dialect

Kiunguja, the Zanzibari dialect, developed as the standard, and such other dialects as Kimvita (spoken in Mombasa) came to be more regionally identified. Mission rivalries played a role in these struggles between Kiunguja and Kimvita.[10] Nowadays, the Swahili that is taught in east African schools and internationally is Standard Swahili, derived from Kiunguja. This policy has tremendous implications for people who speak other Swahili dialects as a first language.

One of the fourteen or so dialects of Swahili, Kimvita is situated right in the middle of the Swahili dialect continuum. It has features from both the northern and southern dialects. It is the dialect spoken mainly by people on Mombasa Island whose first language is Swahili.

From the speech of the three women whose life histories are included here, we see that the Kimvita dialect is moving from pure Kimvita toward a more standardized form of Swahili. The editors decided to present the Swahili text in its original spoken form so that one could see these changes and be able to see how spoken Kimvita contrasts with both written Kimvita and with Standard Swahili.

The following are the main sound changes that occur between Standard Swahili and Kimvita:

Standard Swahili	Kimvita	
ch	t (th)	kichwa--kitwa
nj	nd	njoo----ndoo
nyw	ny	nywele--nyɔle
nyw	nwa	kunywa--kunwa

Conversational Kimvita has a tendency to contract its relative markers (*aliyesubutu* = *alosubutu*), subject prefixes (*nitakwenda* = *ntakwenda*), and tense markers (*sitaki* = *staki, ninataka* = *ntaka*). All three texts exhibit this pattern.

Kimvita speakers use -n- tense in place of -li- and -me-. One can determine which is being substituted by the context. Bi Kaje, the oldest of the three speakers and the one with the least amount of exposure outside the community, does not use -li- or -me-. Instead she uses -n- (*"Babangu anzaliwa hapa Mombasa"* for -li-; *"Maana mzungu hana kabila ya Kiafrika basi akiwa ansilimu huwa ni Mwarabu kwa kuwa hana damu ya Kiswahili"* for -me-). At times Bi Kaje deletes the -me- tense altogether (*"Wao washakufa"*). Shamsa Muhashamy, on the other hand, used the -li- and -me- tenses continuously. Mishi wa Abdala uses all three.

In addition to the above grammatical differences, Kimvita vocabulary differs from Standard. In the cases listed in the glossary, this involves words unique to Kimvita (e.g., *sini*) or words that are pronounced differently but do not follow regular sound changes (e.g., *-swali* for *-sali, shikio* for *sikio*). Finally, Kimvita speakers select one word over another, where both have the same meaning and both are also Standard Swahili (e.g., *-twaa* instead of *-shika*).

In spoken Kimvita the concord agreements are not strictly adhered to, e.g., Bi Kaje says, *"pesa ya kuuzwa kofia zawekwa."* Ma Mishi says, *"Huko kwa Waarabu huko liko shamba la mtu mmoja vile vile yauzwa."* Shamsa Muhashamy says, *"Alitoka hapa hapa Mombasa, lakini yeye ilikuwa ni watu wa Kibokoni."*

All three women are native speakers of Kimvita, yet their subdialects vary. First and foremost, their speech is influenced by the age of the speakers, level of education, and interaction beyond the immediate community of Kimvita speakers.

Bi Kaje is the oldest of the three women. She has had no Western schooling and has the least amount of interaction with speakers outside her community of Twelve Tribes people. Her speech is closest to the "original" Kimvita dialect. She uses older and more Arabic vocabulary, e.g., *sitashara* instead of *kumi na sita*. The English-derived vocabulary in her speech consists of such words as *fruti*, which are well integrated into and considered part of Swahili. This pattern of usage results from her minimal exposure to Western culture and absence of Western education. In the same way, she does not use "foreigner talk" in her conversations with Margaret Strobel or imitate any "foreigner talk." That is, she does not switch from Kimvita to Standard Swahili for the benefit of a non-Kimvita listener. She uses more locative markers in her speech than the other two women. Her speech does not include any -me-tenses; instead she uses the -n- tense. Using the older Kimvita form, she sometimes changes both the first person singular marker ni- and the habitual marker hu- to ha-, e.g., *hamuuliza* for *nikamuuliza*, or *hawanunua* for *huwanunua*.

Ma Mishi speaks more Standard Swahili, as a result of growing up in the community around the Freretown mission of former slaves and their descendants. For example, she uses both t and ch. She also uses both -me- and -n- tenses. Although she does not use "foreigner talk," her awareness of it is illustrated when she uses "foreigner talk" (uses Standard Swahili) while quoting the missionary Bwana Binns. Ma Mishi uses neither Arabic (as distinguished from Swahiliized Arabic words) nor English vocabulary, as do the other two women. The absence is due to several factors: having been brought up in Kisauni, having no formal education, and having no claims to Arabic ancestry or identification with it.

Shamsa Muhashamy is the youngest and the only woman with some Western education. More than the other two women or most Swahili women in Mombasa, she has interacted outside the traditionally defined sphere of women's activities. This lifestyle is reflected in the language as well as the content of her life history. Her use of Standard Swahili is due not only to education but to her involvement in politics. She Swahiliizes English vocabulary, e.g., *kudraiving* (driving), *mafaundaz* (founders). She also uses Arabic pronunciation for words like *tarekhe*. This form of speech is adopted by Kimvita speakers who wish to appear sophisticated by identifying with Arabic culture, or in Shamsa Muhashamy's case, Arabic ancestry.

The change in language of the three women moves from a form of "pure" Kimvita, to a mixture of Kimvita and Standard, to Standard: from Bi Kaje, the oldest and not educated, to Ma Mishi, who is not educated but is more exposed to other ethnic groups, to Shamsa Muhashamy, who is educated and active in politics and who interacts very much with people from other communities. Among young, educated Kimvita speakers, not represented in these texts, there is a trend toward using more Standard Swahili, which is the result of the education policy noted earlier.

Some comments are helpful regarding the editing and translations of these texts. The information was not always provided sequentially, especially in the case of Bi Kaje and Ma Mishi. Some sentences were in response to questions; hence in places the text reads choppily. In the text and translation, brackets indicate insertions; parentheses indicate the woman's parenthetic comments. In translating and to a lesser extent in editing, redundancies were removed. Some expressions that appear redundant in English are not so in Swahili and thus were not omitted in the latter, since the text is intended to mirror spoken language. Swahili does not differentiate by gender, hence "he" and "she," where ambiguous, have been translated into the colloquial English usage "they," or, occasionally in the case of a child of undisclosed gender, "it."

In the Swahili texts, English words are written as they sound in Swahili, with the English version footnoted. Swahili names are spelled phonetically unless spelled otherwise by the person her/himself. Finally, both -mw- and -mu- have been used, since there is no standard way of writing these, e.g., *alimwona* and *alimuona*.

NOTES

Preface

1. Published as *Wanawake Watatu Waswahili wa Mombasa, Kenya* (Bloomington: Indiana University Press, 1989).
2. (New Haven, Conn.: Yale University Press, 1979).

Introduction

1. R. D. Theisz, "The Critical Collaboration: Introductions as a Gateway to the Study of Native American Bi-Autobiography," *American Indian Culture and Research Journal* 5, no. 1 (1981), 65-80.
2. Marcia Wright, "Women in Peril: A Commentary on the Life Stories of Captives in Nineteenth-Century East-Central Africa," *African Social Research* 20 (1975), 800-19. A more extensive version is *Women in Peril* (Lusaka: NECZAM, 1984). See also Marcia Wright, "Since 'Women in Peril': Reconsiderations of Biography, Autobiography and Life Stories of Some African Women with Special Reference to Marriage," paper presented at a conference on "Autobiographies, Biographies and Life Histories of Women: Interdisciplinary Perspectives," University of Minnesota, May 23-24, 1986.
3. Edward A. Alpers, "The Story of Swema: Female Vulnerability in Nineteenth-Century East Africa," in *Women and Slavery in Africa*, ed. Claire C. Robertson and Martin A. Klein (Madison: University of Wisconsin Press, 1983), pp. 185-219.
4. (1954; New Haven and London: Yale University Press, 1981). For a thorough anthropological discussion of life histories, see L. L. Langness and Gelya Frank, *Lives: An Anthropological Approach to Biography* (Novato, Calif.: Chandler and Sharp Publishers, Inc., 1981).
5. Susan N. G. Geiger has pointed out the patriarchal bias of this introduction in "Women's Life Histories: Method and Content," *Signs* 11, no. 2 (1986), 341-42.
6. (Cambridge: Harvard University Press, 1981). Additional

discussion of the process of doing this work is found in Marjorie Shostak, "What the Wind Won't Take Away: Methodological and Ethical Considerations of the Oral History of a Hunting-Gathering Woman," paper presented at a conference on "Autobiographies, Biographies and Life Histories of Women: Interdisciplinary Perspectives," University of Minnesota, May 23-24, 1986.

7. Clyde Kluckhohn, "The Personal Document in Anthropological Science," in *The Use of Personal Documents in History, Anthropology and Sociology*, by Louis Gottschalk, Clyde Kluckhohn, and Robert Angell, Bulletin 53 (New York: Social Science Research Council, 1945), p. 152. See also Theisz, and Lawrence C. Watson, "Understanding a Life History as a Subjective Document: Hermeneutical and Phenomenological Perspectives," *Ethos* 4, no. 1 (Spring 1976), 95-131.

8. "Introduction," *Interpreting Women's Lives: Feminist Theory and Personal Narrative*, ed. the Personal Narratives Group (Bloomington, Ind.: forthcoming 1989).

9. For more detail on the process and relationship, see Margaret Strobel, "Doing Oral History as an Outsider," *Frontiers: A Journal of Women's Studies* 2, no. 2 (1977), 68-72, in the special issue on women's oral history. A second special issue on women's oral history came out as *Frontiers, A Journal of Women's Studies* 7, no. 1 (1983). Strobel's individual collection process contrasts with the more collective and politicized approach described in Marjorie Mbilinyi, "Politics of Personal Narratives," paper presented at a conference on "Autobiographies, Biographies and Life Histories of Women: Interdisciplinary Perspectives," University of Minnesota, May 23-24, 1986.

10. An English version of Ma Mishi's life appeared as "The Life History of Mishi wa Abdala, a Swahili Kungwi from Mombasa, Kenya," *The African Review* 11, no. 1 (1984), 68-80.

11. Harriet Wrye and Jacqueline Churcilla, "Looking Inward, Looking Backward: Reminiscence and the Life Review," *Frontiers: A Journal of Women's Studies* 2, no. 2 (1977), 98-105.

12. (New Haven and London: Yale University Press, 1979).

13. (Washington, D.C.: University Press of America, 1979) with Thomas Hinnebusch.

14. For historical background, see Strobel, *Muslim Women*, Chapter 1; F. J. Berg, "The Swahili Community of Mombasa, 1500-1900," *Journal of African History* 9, no. 1 (1968), 35-56; C. S. Nichols, *The Swahili Coast: Politics, Diplomacy and Trade on the East African Littoral, 1798-1856*, St. Anthony's College, Oxford, Publications no. 2 (London: George Allen and Unwin, 1971); A. I. Salim, *The Swahili-Speaking Peoples of Kenya's Coast, 1895-1965* (Nairobi: East African Publishing House, 1973).

15. See Berg; Fred James Berg, "Mombasa under the Busaidi Sultanate: The City and Its Hinterland in the Nineteenth Century," Ph.D. dissertation, University of Wisconsin, 1971.

16. Edward A. Alpers, *Ivory and Slaves: Changing Patterns of*

International Trade to the Late Nineteenth Century (Berkeley and Los Angeles: University of California Press, 1975); Frederick Cooper, Plantation Slavery on the East Coast of Africa (New Haven and London: Yale University Press, 1977).

17. Hamed bin Saleh El-Busaidy, Ndoa na Talaka [Marriage and Divorce] (Nairobi: East African Literature Bureau, 1958), pp. 7-8.

18. Edward Steere, Swahili Tales, as Told by the Natives of Zanzibar (London: Bell and Daldy, 1870), footnote, p. 490; Derek Nurse and Thomas Spear, The Swahili: Reconstructing the History and Language of an African Society (Philadelphia: University of Pennsylvania Press, 1984), p. 23. For additional evidence see Strobel, Muslim Women, pp. 91-93.

19. Linda Wiley Donley, "House Power: Swahili Space and Symbolic Markers," in Symbolic and Structural Archaeology, ed. Ian Hodder (Cambridge: Cambridge University Press, 1982), p. 68.

20. Strobel, Muslim Women, p. 88, note 122.

21. See Strobel, Muslim Women, pp. 57-58.

22. Marc J. Swarz, "The Isolation of Men and the Happiness of Women: Sources and Use of Power in Swahili Marital Relationships," Journal of Anthropological Research 38 (1982), 34, notes without citing a source that presently one-third of all marriages end in divorce, 60 of these in the first five years. He also identifies an ideal of romantic love in the contemporary Swahili community.

23. Marc J. Swarz, "Culture and Implicit Power: Maneuvers and Understandings in Swahili Nuclear Family Relations," in Culture and Political Change, ed. Myron J. Aronoff (New Brunswick, N.J.: Transaction Books, 1983), pp. 19-38.

24. R. E. S. Tanner and D. F. Roberts, "A Demographic Study in an Area of Low Fertility in North-east Tanganyika," Population Studies 13 (1959-1960), 61-80; and Mtoro bin Mwinyi Bakari, The Customs of the Swahili People: The Desturi za Waswahili of Mtoro bin Mwinyi Bakari and Other Swahili Persons, ed. and trans. J. W. T. Allen (Berkeley: University of California Press, 1981), p. 18. In contrast to this view, Patricia Romero says large surviving slave families were "not unusual," perhaps because of the good fish and fruit diet, "Mama Khadija," in Life Histories of African Women, ed. Patricia W. Romero (London and Atlantic Highlands, N.J.: The Ashfield Press, 1987), p. 142.

25. Kenya, Ministry of Finance and Economic Planning, Statistical Division, Kenya Population Census 1969, Vol. III (Nairobi: Government Printer, 1970), p. 50, Table 2.

26. Leo Silberman, "The Social Survey of the Old Town of Mombasa," Journal of African Administration 2 (January 1950), 14-21.

27. Swarz confirms this in "Isolation." For a discussion of lesbianism, see Gill Shepherd, "Rank, Gender, and Homosexuality: Mombasa as a Key to Understanding Sexual Options," in The Cultural Construction of Sexuality, ed. Pat Caplan (London and New

York: Tavistock Publications, 1987), 240-70.

28. T. O. Ranger, *Dance and Society in Eastern Africa, 1890-1970: The Beni Ngoma* (Berkeley: University of California Press, 1975). For more information on *lelemama*, see Marjorie Ann Franken, "Anyone Can Dance: A Survey and Analysis of Swahili Ngoma, Past and Present," Ph.D. dissertation, University of California, Riverside, 1986.

29. See Ranger, *Dance*, and Peter Lienhardt, "Introduction," in *The Medicine Man, Swifa ya Nguvumali*, by Hasani bin Ismail, ed. and trans. Peter Lienhardt (London: Oxford University Press, 1968); Mtoro bin Mwinyi Bakari, pp. 83-84.

30. That is to say, none of the women mentioned *pepo* cults, and Strobel does not recall inquiring directly. See Farouk Mohamedhussein Tharia Topan, "Oral Literature in a Ritual Setting: The Role of Spirit Songs in a Spirit-Mediumship Cult of Mombasa, Kenya," Ph.D. dissertation, University of London, 1971; for the Comoro Islands, see Michael Lambek, *Human Spirits: A Cultural Account of Trance in Mayotte* (Cambridge and New York: Cambridge University Press, 1981); and the dissertation in progress of Linda Lavinia Giles, Department of Anthropology, University of Texas at Austin, "Spirit Possession on Swahili Coast," which research is the basis for "Possession Cults on the Swahili Coast: A Re-examination of Theories of Marginality," *Africa* 57, no. 2 (1987), 234-58.

Part I: Kaje wa Mwenye Matano
Introduction

1. The social status of children of concubines was not necessarily less than that of the child of two freeborn parents. Frederick Cooper notes their equality in the Malindi area to the north of Mombasa and along the Kenya coast to the south, *Plantation Slavery on the East Coast of Africa* (New Haven: Yale University Press, 1977), p. 197. For Lamu there is disagreement. Abdul Hamid M. el-Zein claims inequality in *The Sacred Meadows: A Structural Analysis of Religion Symbolism in an East African Town* (Evanston, Ill.: Northwestern University Press, 1974), pp. 31-33. Patricia Romero Curtin disputes this claim in "Laboratory for the Oral History of Slavery: The Island of Lamu on the Kenya Coast," *American Historical Review* 88, no. 4 (October 1983), p. 870, note 38.

2. Pat Caplan, "Gender, Ideology and Modes of Production on the Coast of East Africa," *Paideuma* 28 (1982), pp. 36-37.

3. James de Vere Allen, "Swahili Culture Reconsidered: Some Historical Implications of the Material Culture of the Northern Kenya Coast in the Eighteenth and Nineteenth Centuries," *Azania* 9 (1974), 105-37.

4. This phenomenon is also noted in M. G. Smith, "Introduction," in *Baba of Karo: A Woman of the Muslim Hausa*, by Mary F. Smith

(1954; rpt. New Haven and London: Yale University Press, 1981), p. 13.

5. Cooper, *Plantation Slavery*, Chapter 5, especially p. 176.

6. These tables are found also in Margaret Strobel, "Slavery and Reproductive Labor in Mombasa," in Claire C. Robertson and Martin A. Klein, *Women and Slavery in Africa* (Madison: University of Wisconsin Press, 1983), pp. 111-29. Not all the data from which these tables are derived are present in the narrative. Some were in response to direct questions and not easily integrated into the story.

7. "Women's Importance in African Slave Systems," in *Women and Slavery in Africa*, p. 16.

8. Marcia Wright, "Women in Peril: A Commentary upon the Life Stories of Captives in Nineteenth-Century East Central Africa," *African Social Research* 20 (December 1975), pp. 805, 818. This is implied also in Patricia Romero Curtin, "Laboratory for the Oral History of Slavery: The Island of Lamu on the Kenya Coast," *American Historical Review* 88, no. 4 (October 1983), p. 880.

9. See Margaret Strobel, *Muslim Women in Mombasa, 1890-1975* (New Haven and London: Yale University Press, 1979), pp. 51-54; Curtin, "Laboratory," p. 869, note 34.

10. Curtin, "Laboratory," p. 872; Cooper, *Plantation Slavery*, p. 225.

11. "Female Slavery," in *Women and Slavery in Africa*, pp. 51-55.

12. R. E. S. Tanner and D. F. Roberts, "A Demographic Study in an Area of Low Fertility in North-east Tanganyika," *Population Studies* 13 (1959-60), 61-80; Mtoro bin Mwinyi Bakari, *The Customs of the Swahili People: The Desturi za Waswahili of Mtoro bin Mwinyi Bakari and Other Swahili Persons*, ed. and trans. J. W. T. Allen (Berkeley: University of California Press, 1981), p. 18.

13. Curtin, "Laboratory"; Patricia W. Romero, "'Where Have All the Slaves Gone?' Emancipation and Post-emancipation in Lamu, Kenya," *Journal of African History* 27, no. 3 (1986), 497-512; Cooper, *Plantation Slavery*.

14. Strobel, *Muslim Women*, pp. 73-76; M. G. Smith, p. 22.

My Family

1. Bi Kaje initially identified her mother, Ndaasili, as the wife of her father. In a later interview she indicated Ndaasili was a concubine. Notably, Bi Kaje knows little of her mother's background, and Ndaasili drops out of her narrative at an early stage. Bi Kaje's lack of knowledge about her mother probably stems from several sources. She was raised by her grandmothers Mwana Mjomvu and Bi Nyanya, and slaves raised two of her siblings. Customarily the first child was raised by its paternal grandmother; the second, by its maternal grandmother if she was freeborn. (This practice continues today.) In addition to being raised by grandmothers, Bi Kaje lost her mother at age seven.

Still, her absence of knowledge about Ndaasili derives in part from the latter's low status.

2. Bi Hindi is described as Bi Kaje's father's mother's sibling or cousin. Elsewhere she is said to be related to Bi Kaje's father's mother's mother, Binti Kombo. But the precise relationship is unclear.

3. The word in the Swahili text, *marekani*, was a generic term for cloth that derived from trade with the United States. Not all *marekani* was American-made cloth.

4. It is difficult to place Bi Hindi precisely in the economic hierarchy of Mombasa. She may, as Bi Kaje claims, not have been enormously rich, but she appears to have been wealthier than other Three Tribes (or even Twelve Tribes) members. We do not know the acreage of the two farms she owned. According to Frederick Cooper's figures for landownership around the turn of the century in Kisauni (not Changamwe, where Bi Hindi's farms lay), the average Three Tribes person owned less than the average acreage, calculated by including all ethnic groups. Thus, by this standard, Bi Hindi with two farms might hold slightly above the average amount of land. In owning twenty-five of the thirty slaves associated with the household described below, Bi Hindi appears to have far exceeded the average. Cooper found that "some planters had two slaves, some six. One of the wealthiest Swahili landowners of all reputedly had forty." *Plantation Slavery on the East Coast of Africa* (New Haven: Yale University Press, 1977), p. 103.

5. This classification suggests the relative importance of religion over race in defining people's status as well as the outsider status of both Arabs and Europeans.

6. Bi Kaje claims to be a member of the Changamwe, part of the Three Tribes section of the Twelve Tribes, drawing upon her great-grandmother Binti Kombo being Changamwe, since her (Bi Kaje's) father's father (Msumbeni) was of Shirazi background.

7. Derek Nurse and Thomas Spear suggest that people use "Shirazi" ancestry to identify with a historical Swahili group that represents culturally a maritime, Islamic, patrilineal, stratified, and heterogeneous society. *The Swahili: Reconstructing the History and Language of an African Society* (Philadelphia: University of Pennsylvania Press, 1984), pp. 74-79. Before the twentieth century, the Shirazi were thought to be immigrants to the Swahili coast from Persia. (The capital of Fars was Shiraz.) Historians now believe that few of these immigrants were actually Persian, that instead they came from Persian-controlled parts of Arabia to the Swahili coast and established a significant dynasty in Mogadishu in the thirteenth century. From there they migrated south and established ruling dynasties in Kilwa (thirteenth century) and Mombasa (fourteenth century). The Shirazi dynasty in Mombasa was associated with Sheik Mvita, replacing a non-Shirazi dynasty founded by a woman, Mwana Mkisi. (Celebrations at Sheik Mvita's grave are described by Bi Kaje in "Childhood.") Nowadays, claims

to Shirazi heritage are used to imply "noble or at least nonservile ancestry." Fred James Berg, "Mombasa under the Busaidi Sultanate: The City and Its Hinterland in the Nineteenth Century," Ph.D. dissertation (University of Wisconsin, 1971), p. 24. See also chapters by H. Neville Chittick, "The Coast before the Arrival of the Portuguese," and F. J. Berg, "The Coast from the Portuguese Invasion to the Rise of the Zanzibar Sultanate," in B. A. Ogot, *Zamani: A Survey of East African History* (1968; 2nd ed., Nairobi: East African Publishing House, 1973), pp. 98-114 and 115-134 respectively; H. Neville Chittick, "The Shirazi Colonization of East Africa," *Journal of African History* 6, no. 3 (1965), 275-94.

8. People from the Comoro Islands speak a dialect of Swahili and share many aspects of Swahili mainland culture. See Gill Shepherd, "Two Marriage Forms in the Comoro Islands: An Investigation," *Africa* 47, no. 4 (1977), 344-59.

9. A *sharifu* is a person who claims decent from the Prophet. *Masharifu* (pl.) are honored, respected, consulted on important personal or community matters, and sometimes given daughters in marriage. For the latter, see Patricia Romero Curtin, "Laboratory for the Oral History of Slavery: The Island of Lamu on the Kenya Coast," *American Historical Review* 88, no. 4 (October 1983), 858-82.

Slavery

1. Land Office records show a sale of land in Changamwe by a person named Kaje to a Ugandan in 1904. Land Office Register, Vol. A16, 1904, entry #56. I thank Frederick Cooper for sharing his data from these registers. Whether or not this is land that belonged to Kaje wa Mwenye Matano is uncertain. She did not recognize the Ugandan name or transaction, but one would not expect recognition if her guardian sold it without her knowledge. Kaje is not a common name, so this sale might indeed have been her inheritance. Although it is hard to determine how commonly minors lost property in this manner, her experience was not unique. In 1896 one Binti Seleman bin Jabu complained to the colonial administrator "Bwana Crauford" that her uncle took her father's entire estate and $700 of her share because she was "small." Kenya National Archives, Coast 1, 67/14, letter #42.

2. Since slaves were not given the names of the Prophet or His descendants, this name marks Saidi's movement away from his slave ancestry and his integration into the household.

3. Bi Izhe is identified in a text not included here as Bi Kaje's *shangazi* (father's sister) and as Mwenye Matano's *ndugu kwa mama wa pili* (half-sister by another mother). This is confusing, since his father is Msumbeni and Bi Izhe's father is Mwenzagu wa Mwenye Hija. If they have both different mothers and different fathers, it is hard to see how they can be half-siblings. There is obviously a close relationship that we cannot precisely identify.

4. The Liwali was the highest Muslim official; the position was retained by the colonial administration. For references to Salim bin Khalfan, consult index in Frederick Cooper, *Plantation Slavery on the East Coast of Africa* (New Haven and London: Yale University Press, 1977). His son, Sir Ali bin Salim, was the Liwali for the Coast from 1921 to 1931, the officially recognized Arab leader. See A. I. Salim, "Sir Ali Bin Salim," *Kenya Historical Biographies*, ed. A. I. Salim and Kenneth King, Nairobi Historical Studies, No. 2 (Nairobi: University of Nairobi, 1971), pp. 112-41.

5. The Digo are Mijikenda who live south of Mombasa. Tosha means "enough."

6. Faida means "profit." Her being in purdah, mentioned later, is a sign of high status. Concubines occupied a special status. Under the Shafi'i school of Islamic law followed in Mombasa, a man could not marry his own slave; he had to free her. But he could take unlimited numbers of slave concubines in addition to the four wives to which he was entitled. For a poor man like Bi Kaje's father, concubines provided an inexpensive way to have children, sexual relations, and domestic life, since he could avoid paying wedding gifts of dowry to the woman and her family. Concubines were not freed in 1907 with other slaves. Instead, in 1909 the abolition ordinance was amended to assure continued financial support and to free them under certain conditions.

7. Takosani means *"nitakosa nini?"*, "what wrong will I do if I do good to someone?"

8. Hakuna means "there is nothing."

9. A *fundi* is a skilled person.

10. The Giriama are Mijikenda. The archives describe several cases of Giriama women running away to the coast and marrying Muslim men, which became an issue in particular in 1919. Kenya National Archives, Coast 1/24/243.

11. According to Bi Kaje, Majaliwa means "something happens to me, but that's fine. That is how God intended it to be for me."

12. The Chonyi are Mijikenda.

13. Afua means "deliverance."

14. Baheri relates to *heri*, or "good fortune." *Riziki* are necessities. Maburuki derives from *baraka*, "blessing."

15. Twafuateje and her son Faraji are mentioned two paragraphs above.

16. The Yao live in southern Tanzania and northern Mozambique. Hatimjawe means "God doesn't desert his creation," *haati mja wake.*

17. The Kamba live in east-central Kenya.

18. Noeza means "He has taught me." Bi Kaje explains, "If you do something and you get really tired of it, and then the discomfort goes away, then you think, 'Ah, God has taught me a lesson now.'"

19. These *leso* are colorful cloths worn in pairs by women.

20. The Ngindo live in southern Tanzania.

21. The Nyamwezi live in central Tanzania. The *eda*, or period

of mourning, is four months and ten days.

22. The Khojas are South Asian Shia Muslims. They include both Ithnasharis and Ismailis.

23. The Bohoras are South Asian Shia Muslims. See Hakim Amiji, "The Bohoras of East Africa," *Journal of Religion in Africa* (1976), 27-40.

24. The Duruma are Mijikenda.

25. The Chonyi are Mijikenda.

26. The colonial government dredged a deep-water port at Kilindini on the western side of the island. Traditional dhow traffic continued at the port in Old Town.

27. Bi Kaje distinguishes gifts from a husband as "her own," as opposed to gifts from her mother/aunt. Perhaps these slaves were purchased as her husband's wedding gifts to her, which belong to her, in distinction from the wedding gifts to her parents.

28. Sikukuu means "holiday." Asmini is jasmine. Kishindo means "outburst, shock."

29. The name Mahia is not commonly used.

30. Mtenzi is someone who looks after things. Hidaya means "gift." For the Hidaya Mosque, see F. J. Berg and B. J. Walter, "Mosques, Population and Urban Development in Mombasa," *Hadith 1* (1968), pp. 74-75.

31. The Kami live in central Tanzania.

32. Mefaida's life resembles that of Hatimjawe, mentioned earlier. It is possible that Bi Kaje has confused them.

33. Bi Kaje identifies a person Makutubu as the agent of the 1907 abolition, perhaps the individual or individuals who processed claims. The word derives from the words for contract *(mkataba)* and clerk *(katibu)*. This term is not commonly used elsewhere, nor was it familiar to other people in Mombasa who were queried. Frederick Cooper heard the term used in Malindi and suggests that some people intended it to apply to Kenneth MacDougall, who was appointed Registrar of Slaves and who supervised the courts that carried out the work of freeing the slaves. Personal communication.

34. The Chagga live in northern Tanzania.

35. Baadadhiki means "after stress comes relief."

Childhood

1. It is unclear who the Hindoko and Hindeo are. Edward Alpers suggests that Hindoko might be Sikhs.

2. 35 lbs.

3. Note that women as well as men gave religious instruction. Saidi may be the *mzalia* in Bi Hindi's household.

4. The Ghazali Private Muslim School was taken over by the government after two or three years in 1938. The curriculum included religious training, Arabic, Swahili, the usual secular subjects, and domestic science. Although the curriculum clearly intended to train girls to be better wives and mothers, some women

went on to take jobs. Initially teaching was the preferred occupation, but by the 1960s such other jobs as clerical work were being filled by Swahili women. In a sense the concern that education would lead to a breakdown in norms of modesty and seclusion was well founded. But the causes of these changes were more complex and profound than could be attributed to education alone, including the immigration of large members of non-Muslims to Mombasa and the assaults of Western values and culture under colonialism. For education and employment, see Margaret Strobel, *Muslim Women in Mombasa, 1890-1975* (New Haven and London: Yale University Press, 1979), Chapter 4.

5. As the celebration of the Prophet's birthday, Maulidi is a traditional Islamic holiday. Mombasa's celebration was not as extravagant or popular as those in Lamu or Malindi, to which coastal people came in droves. Women might celebrate in their homes, reading the appropriate Koranic verses and serving special foods. For a detailed description of the Lamu Maulidi, see Abdul Hamid el-Zein, *The Sacred Meadows: A Structural Analysis of Religious Symbolism in an East African Town* (Evanston, Ill.: Northwestern University Press, 1974), Chapter 8.

6. For a discussion of the complex situation of European women in the colonies, see Margaret Strobel, "Gender and Race in the Nineteenth- and Twentieth-Century British Empire," in *Becoming Visible: Women in European History*, ed. Renate Bridenthal, Claudia Koonz, and Susan Stuard (Boston: Houghton Mifflin, 1987), 375-96.

7. The Swahili New Year, *Siku ya Mwaka* (not January 1), represents a local practice to which Islamic elements have been attached. John Milner Gray, "*Nairuz* or *Siku ya Mwaka*," *Tanganyika Notes and Records* 38 (1955), 1-22.

8. The circulation of the bull described by Bi Kaje is performed in other Swahili towns as well, notably Lamu. Its purpose is to purify the town by offering a sacrifice. The town's pollution, in the form of the bones and refuse, is eliminated by being thrown into the ocean. Bi Kaje attributes bad occurrences in Mombasa to the failure of people to perform the ritual properly. For the ritual in Lamu, see El-Zein, *Sacred Meadows*, Chapter 7.

9. As Pat Caplan notes, one finds more female participation in these customary activities, which reflect *mila* (custom) rather than *sheria* (Islamic law). Indeed, women are central to the *gungu* dance performed at the grave of Sheik Mvita, who is associated with the Shirazi dynasty that ruled Mombasa from approximately the fourteenth to the sixteenth centuries. "Gender, Ideology and Modes of Production on the Coast of East Africa," *Paideuma* 28 (1982), 29-43.

Although Bi Kaje has not attended the *gungu* dance, her description of it coincides with written representations and performances witnessed in the mid-1970s. See Edward Steere, *Swahili Tales, as Told by the Natives of Zanzibar* (London: Bell and Daldy, 1870), pp. 474-83.

10. The Kilifi are one of the Nine Tribes. Sheik Mvita was associated with the Nine Tribes.

11. The Wamiji (s., Mmiji; abstract form, *umiji*) whom Bi Kaje described played a greater role in society than she acknowledges. Their activities often related to kinship, involving rituals at weddings and funerals, and involved self-help. See Strobel, *Muslim Women*, pp. 80-81. They may be analogous to the male and female elders described at the turn of the century along the Tanzanian coast. See Mtoro bin Mwinyi Bakari, *The Customs of the Swahili People: The Desturi za Waswahili of Mtoro bin Mwinyi Bakari and Other Swahili Persons*, ed. and trans. J. W. T. Allen (Berkeley: University of California Press, 1981), p. 439.

12. This is Bi Kaje's phrase spoken in English.

13. Cousins of the opposite sexes are not allowed to mix, because they are preferred marriage partners.

14. Mackinnon Market is the large, main market on the edge of Old Town.

Husbands and Children

1. Although this event occurs following abolition, Bi Kaje still describes Tabia as Muhamadi's slave.

2. The influence of purdah is seen in Bi Kaje's use of intermediaries, first her brother, later her ex-slave nanny Baadadhiki, and finally her uncle who collects from the judge the payments due to her from her husband.

3. Because of Swahili kinship terminology, it is not clear whether or not the grandmother who secretly aids her is the same grandmother who refused to harbor her physically. If so, she is sending Bi Kaje back to her husband to avoid legal hassles. Also, in Swahili culture, relatives try to discourage marital breakups.

4. In the first set of interviews done in 1972-73, Bi Kaje omitted mention of her second husband, Ali. Perhaps she found the memory particularly painful; perhaps she felt more trusting and comfortable discussing very personal matters during the second set of interviews two years later.

5. The eldest child, Ahmadi, died at about eight months.

6. Incoherent with anger, Bi Kaje is making the point that the second wife does not get clothes from her husband: he does not support her as a husband should.

7. Swahili pastries.

8. For more on midwifery and childbirth, see Mbarak bin Ali Hinawiy, "Notes on Customs in Mombasa," *Swahili* 34, pt. 1 (1964), 17-35; Patricia Romero, "Mama Khadija," in *Life Histories of African Women*, ed. Patricia W. Romero (London and Atlantic Highlands, N.J.: The Ashfield Press, 1987), pp. 152-54.

9. For a discussion of the role of women like Mrs. Anthony, see Margaret Strobel, "Gender and Race in the Nineteenth- and Twentieth-Century British Empire," in *Becoming Visible, Women in*

European History, ed. Renate Bridenthal, Claudia Koonz, and Susan Stuard (Boston: Houghton Mifflin, 1987), 375-96.

10. The symptom is convulsions. *Babu* is thought to be caused by an owl settling on the roof of the house; Frederick Johnson, *A Standard Swahili-English Dictionary* (1939; rpt. London: Oxford University Press, 1967); Mtoro bin Mwinyi Bakari, *The Customs of the Swahili People: The Desturi za Waswahili of Mtoro bin Mwinyi Bakari and Other Swahili Persons*, ed. and trans. J. W. T. Allen (Berkeley: University of California Press, 1981), p. 14.

11. See Mtoro bin Mwinyi Bakari, *Customs*, pp. 45-54, for circumcision on the northern Tanzanian coast at a similar period; A. P. Caplan, "Boys' Circumcision and Girls' Puberty Rites among the Swahili of Mafia Island," *Africa* 46, no. 1 (1976), 21-33.

12. Many slaves came from these east-central African societies, which had puberty rites. See Margaret Strobel, *Muslim Women in Mombasa, 1890-1975* (New Haven and London: Yale University Press, 1979), Chapter 8.

13. This name is not commonly used.

14. For more discussion of rural vs. urban culture, see James de Vere, Allen, "Town and Country in Swahili Culture," in *Perspectives des Études Africaines Contemporaines* (Cologne: Deutsche UNESCO-Kommission, 1974), pp. 298-316.

Adult Life

1. The right to perform a particular ritual or dance marked social status in the nineteenth century. Bi Kaje claimed, whether true or not, that the Tangana have been forbidden to beat the large drum *(goma kuu)* ever since they allowed a *"hadimu"* (a slave) to beat it on one occasion. Only the remaining members of the Three Tribes, the Changamwe and the Kilindini, are allowed to beat the large drum.

2. From King.

3. For the parallel men's bands known as *bwaride, gwaride,* or *beni,* see T. O. Ranger, *Dance and Society in Eastern Africa, 1890-1970: The Beni Ngoma* (Berkeley: University of California Press, 1975).

4. Carol A. Campbell and Carol M. Eastman, *"Ngoma:* Swahili Adult Song Performance in Context," *Ethnomusicology* 28, no. 3 (September 1984), 467-93, has a discussion of various dances, including *chakacha.*

5. From Scotch.

6. People give (pay for) a performance by a men's *beni* or women's dance group as a gift.

7. The presence of Italian prisoners of war distinguished World War Two.

8. It is unclear who the Mahindoo and Mazula are. Susan Geiger suggested they might be Indian and South African (Zulu) troops, but this seems unlikely. In Swahili "Hindu" would be pronounced

with an "u," not with two "o" sounds.

9. For more information, see Geoffrey Hodges, *The Carrier Corps: Military Labor in the East African Campaign, 1914-1918* (Westport, Conn.: Greenwood Press, 1986).

10. The Swahili text uses the word *boi*, from the colonial "boy," rather than the nonderogatory term *mtumishi*.

11. Fatu is Ma Zuena's daughter. Her brother, Mbarak bin Ali Hinawiy, became Liwali in 1936. See A. I. Salim, *The Swahili-Speaking Peoples of Kenya's Coast, 1895-1965* (Nairobi: East African Publishing House, 1973), p. 203 and *passim* for the rest of his career.

12. Bi Kaje chose to live with a female friend because she did not get along with various relatives and was soured on marriage. Such households of women are not uncommon.

13. Mtoro bin Mwinyi Bakari, *The Customs of the Swahili People: The Desturi za Waswahili of Mtoro bin Mwinyi Bakari and Other Swahili Persons*, ed. and trans. J. W. T. Allen (Berkeley: University of California Press, 1981), pp. 118-19. A traditional female craft, weaving is still done, for both local and tourist consumption.

14. Jigija is something black.

15. Her anecdote about Pereira's wife illustrates the cosmopolitan nature of Mombasa and the racial/social stratification of colonial society. It is striking that Bi Kaje recalls Pereira sending out invitations for his wife's funeral to various ethnic groups--Europeans, Mazruis, Omanis, Swahilis--each in their own mail bag. This categorization likely represents her own classification system more than the reality of the events. And she describes the procession with Europeans first, followed by Pereira's own ethnic group, Goans.

16. The incident between Pereira's wife and Bi Kaje's children reveals the necessary accommodations that people of different cultural and religious backgrounds had to make with one another, perhaps more successfully in this instance than was usually the case.

Part II: Mishi wa Abdala
Introduction

1. Frederick Cooper, *Plantation Slavery on the East Coast of Africa* (New Haven and London: Yale University Press, 1977), p. 115.

2. Cooper, *Plantation*, p. 120.

3. Norman R. Bennett, "The Church Missionary Society at Mombasa, 1873-1894," *Boston University Papers in African History* 1 (1964), 171. For a description of Freretown, see James Mbotela, *The Freeing of the Slaves* (London: Evans Brothers, 1956).

4. For further discussion and interpretation of the puberty rites, see Margaret Strobel, *Muslim Women in Mombasa, 1890-1975* (New Haven and London: Yale University Press, 1979), Chapter 8.

5. See Victor Turner, *The Ritual Process: Structure and Anti-structure* (London: Routledge and Kegan Paul, 1969); *The Drums of Affliction: A Study of Religious Processes among the Ndembu of Zambia* (Oxford: Clarendon Press, 1968); *The Forest of Symbols: Aspects of Ndembu Ritual* (Ithaca, N.Y.: Cornell University Press, 1967).

6. Pat Caplan, "Gender, Ideology and Modes of Production on the Coast of East Africa," *Paideuma* 28 (1982), 29-43. In her comments to us, Fatma Husein suggested that *sheria* allows some rights to women that Islamic *mila* denies; that is, women have used *sheria* to claim more equal treatment.

7. For further discussion, see Strobel, *Muslim Women*, Chapter 1.

8. For the freeborn rituals, see Mbarak bin Ali Hinawiy, "Notes on Customs in Mombasa," *Swahili* 34, pt. 1 (1964), 17-35.

9. For the tendency of Swahili communities to divide into factions and rival groups, see Peter Lienhardt, "Introduction," in *The Medicine Man, Swifa ya Nguvumali*, by Hasani bin Ismail, ed. and trans. Peter Lienhardt (London: Oxford University Press, 1968); Mtoro bin Mwinyi Bakari, *The Customs of the Swahili People: The Desturi za Waswahili of Mtoro bin Mwinyi Bakari and Other Swahili Persons*, ed. and trans. J. W. T. Allen (Berkeley: University of California Press, 1981), pp. 83-84, 94-97, and notes; Abdul Hamid el-Zein, *The Sacred Meadows: A Structural Analysis of Religious Symbolism in an East African Town* (Evanston, Ill.: Northwestern University Press, 1974), *passim*, and T. O. Ranger, *Dance and Society in Eastern Africa, 1890-1970: The Beni Ngoma* (Berkeley: University of California Press, 1975), *passim*.

My Family

1. Nemsi is an old Swahili word for honor. The three names, Muslim, Christian, and customary (so-and-so's mother), reflect the cultural diversity of Nancy/Fatuma's background. Ma Mishi was born ca. 1900, apparently the fourth child; her mother was born perhaps ca. 1880 in Kisauni as the eldest, after her parents had married and been captured.

2. Even a woman of Ma Mishi's limited education noted the independence of Mozambique in 1975, about the time of the interview. Since she did not otherwise exhibit a strongly critical attitude toward colonialism, one might speculate that her interest in Mozambique was fed by her ancestors' origins there.

3. The expulsion of Nancy/Fatuma and Albert/Abdala from the mission for fornication is not surprising. When the lay director of the mission, Handford, was arrested in 1886 on similar charges, an African missionary noted the irony. An investigation of the mission conducted by Bishop Tucker in 1892 revealed conditions in the children's dormitories that he described as "not merely a disgrace to the Church Missionary Society but to Christianity itself." Mr. Binns, who is mentioned by Ma Mishi, "described the girls'

dormitory as little more than 'a feeder for the ranks of prostitutes.'" Norman R. Bennett, "The Church Missionary Society at Mombasa, 1873-1894," *Boston University Papers in African History* 1 (1964), 159-95, quote from p. 193. For a description of Freretown, see James Mbotela, *The Freeing of the Slaves* (London: Evans Brothers, 1956).

4. Abdala used to his advantage the familiarity he gained with Europeans' ways at the mission station. His work as a servant and cook is indicative of the greater options for employment available to male ex-slaves. See Marcia Wright, "Women in Peril: A Commentary upon the Life Stories of Captives in Nineteenth-Century East Central Africa," *African Social Research* 20 (December 1975), 805, 818. Ma Mishi's naming of her father's work is characteristic of the colonial milieu. In Swahili she used the term *boi* (boy) instead of the nonderogatory *mtumishi* (servant). Her use of *boi* suggests an uncritical attitude toward colonial relationships, or a lack of awareness of the issue. The question of gender and domestic service is discussed in *Muslim Women in Mombasa, 1890-1975* (New Haven and London: Yale University Press, 1979), pp. 128-31. See also Karen Tranberg Hansen, *Distant Companions: Servants and Employers in Zambia, 1900-1985* (Ithaca, N.Y.: Cornell University Press, 1989).

5. Ma Mishi's description of Thula, her *kungwi*, confirms the ties of Mijikenda groups with Old Town Mombasa residents, either through the traditional *utani* link or through slavery. It is interesting that Thula, though a Mijikenda, practiced *ukungwi* with Nancy. Nancy's *ukungwi* is rooted in the east-central African cultural context, which suggests that Thula may have been a former slave who took on this aspect of slave culture. Ma Mishi uses the term *somo* interchangeably with *kungwi*. People of Bi Kaje's background would associate *kungwi* with slaves, identifying the sexual instructor of elite girls as *somo* only.

6. Binns's easy acceptance of her activities as a *kungwi* was not found everywhere. In contrast, T. O. Ranger has recorded the reaction of missionaries in Masasi, Tanganyika. There, they assimilated male rituals into Christian circumcision rites but did not similarly accommodate female rituals. T. O. Ranger, "Missionary Adaptation of African Religious Institutions: The Masasi Case," in *The Historical Study of African Religions*, ed. T. O. Ranger and Isaria Kimambo (London: Heinemann, 1972), pp. 221-51. Binns was in Rabai in 1879, and in Freretown by 1892. He completed a translation of the New Testament begun by William E. Taylor. It was published in 1909. Joan Russell, *Communicative Competence in a Minority Group: A Sociolinguistic Study of the Swahili-Speaking Community in the Old Town, Mombasa* (Leiden: Brill, 1981), p. 51.

7. For braiding as a female occupation, see Mtoro bin Mwinyi Bakari, *The Customs of the Swahili People: The Desturi za Waswahili of Mtoro bin Mwinyi Bakari and Other Swahili Persons,*

ed. and trans. J. W. T. Allen (Berkeley: University of California Press, 1981), pp. 115-16.

8. Male servants did not like to wash women's underwear. See Buchi Emecheta, *The Joys of Motherhood* (New York: George Braziller, 1979), pp. 49-51.

9. In addition to her daughter Halima, Ma Mishi raised several children, including her niece Jabu, with whom she lived at the time of the interviews.

10. Halima's legs were crippled by polio.

Puberty Rites, Weddings, and *Lelemama*

1. Later, in describing the initiation rites, Ma Mishi mentions *boji*, a beer brewed from millet.

2. People of Ma Mishi's social class use *somo* and *kungwi* interchangeably. Elites associate a *kungwi* with lower-class rituals, *somo* with instruction of elite girls. Note the *kungwi*'s advice: she supports her *mwari*, but in a way that reinforces the husband's role as superior in the marriage.

3. The fact that the knowledgeable Ngariba is her second husband is reminiscent of the weakness of the initial marriage among the Swahili, which is usually arranged by parents.

4. See the *mbura* tree, later in this chapter. Clitoridectomy is not part of the Mombasa rites. *Kutahiri*, used in the Swahili text, means "to cleanse" and may be used to refer to circumcision.

5. The vomiting is for purification.

6. Ma Shea, the senior member of Ma Mishi's group, died between 1973 and 1975.

7. No biological relationship.

8. In the house of a senior *kungwi*, in this case Ma Shea. *Tangalizi*, a food cooked in coconut milk made from seven grains (corn, sesame, millet, rice, *mbaazi* peas, and two kinds of beans-- namely, *kunde* and *maharagwe*), is part of Islamic rituals, the Swahili New Year, and various spirit possession ceremonies. Personal communication, Linda Giles.

9. Perhaps menstrual cloths.

10. The method by which the *makungwi* obtained the *ngondo* dance and the next dance, *mbura*, underscores the links between these rituals and those of peoples who were taken as slaves from Tanzania, Mozambique, and farther inland. In the dance *Ngondo*, which is the Yao word for "war," the initiates try to extract with their teeth a coconut bobbing in a cauldron of boiling water.

11. In this dance the initiates try to hang strands of beads on the whitened *mbura* branch, using only their mouths. Initiates in spirit possession cults also must use only their mouths to perform certain tasks. Personal communication, Linda Giles.

12. The chain dance uses *pembe*, a silver chain. The word means "ivory" in Swahili, reminiscent of the ivory carried by slaves in caravans to the coast in previous centuries. Sharifa Zawawi

suggested in her comments to us that *pembe* might mean "Pemba" and hence not relate to ivory and slaves. See her *Contact and Change: A Study of the East African Coast* (Great Neck, N.Y.: Todd and Honeywell, forthcoming).

13. Fatma Mwaita, the *kungwi* of Ma Mishi's twin sister, Dogo, was queen of the *lelemama* group Banu Saada.

14. Ibinaal Watan is called Ibinaa in speech. For more, see Shamsa Muhamad Muhashamy, under *lelemama*.

15. Sharifa Zawawi suggested an alternative translation: that both Arabs and slaves worked at the dance together, that they danced together.

Part III: Shamsa Muhamad Muhashamy
Introduction

1. Paul Reichard, *Deutsch-Ostafrika: Das Land und Seine Bewohner* (Leipzig: Otto Spamer, 1892); Capt. C. H. Stigand, *The Land of the Zinj* (London: Constable and Co., 1913), p. 122.

2. According to Sharifa Zawawi, *leso* is used in Lamu and Mombasa; *kanga* is used in Mombasa and Tanzania. *Nguo mbili* (two cloths) predated both terms. *Kisutu* may be older than both terms and later developed the specialized meaning of a wedding cloth. "Cloth and the Message in East Africa," unpublished paper, African Studies Association, 1987.

3. See *Mombasa Times*, October 6, 1954, reporting a speech by Sheik Ali bin Namaan. Sheik Al-Amin bin Aly Mazrui also criticized extravagant weddings in 1930 in "Ada Zetu Maarusini" [Our wedding customs], *Uwongozi* (ca. 1932; rpt. Mombasa: East African Muslim Welfare Society, 1955), essay no. 13, p. 23.

4. For an analysis of his life and work, see Randall L. Pouwels, "Sh. Al-Amin b. Ali Mazrui and Islamic Modernism in East Africa, 1875-1947," *International Journal of Middle Eastern Studies* 13 (1981), pp. 329-45.

5. Competition is a common element in Swahili dance, see T. O. Ranger, *Dance and Society in Eastern Africa: The Beni Ngoma* (Berkeley and Los Angeles: University of California Press, 1975), and Peter Lienhardt, "Introduction," *The Medicine Man, Swifa ya Nguvumali*, by Hasani bin Ismail, ed. and trans. Peter Lienhardt (London: Oxford University Press, 1968). For more on *lelemama* and on competition, see Marjorie Ann Franken, "Anyone Can Dance: A Survey and Analysis of Swahili Ngoma, Past and Present," Ph.D. dissertation, University of California, Riverside, 1986, pp. 145-48 and 219-20 respectively.

6. Fatma Husein suggests that *lelemama* groups could have developed into more productive and useful organizations for women. But they became self-destructive in part because by the 1950s, talented (and educated) women had other outlets for their leadership. Private communication, 3-30-88.

My Early Life and Family

1. Note the pattern of being raised by or living with a grandmother.

2. 100,000, an Indian measure, indicative of the Indian influence in commercial matters.

3. Influenced by Egyptian modernists who tried to change Islamic practice in the area of education and the status of women, her father raised her in a fashion that would raise eyebrows today, not to mention in the 1920s. See Albert Hourani, *Arabic Thought in the Liberal Age, 1798-1939* (London: Oxford University Press, 1962).

4. The Mudir is an administrative and judicial office below Liwali. It derived from the earlier Muslim administration and was retained by the British.

5. A Muslim man may marry a woman from groups who have received revealed scriptures, i.e., Christians and Jews, although Reuben Levy states that Shafi'i law, which governs east African Swahili populations, "makes it virtually impossible to wed non-Muslim women." A Muslim woman may not marry a non-Muslim. *The Social Structure of Islam: Being the Second Edition of the Sociology of Islam* (1957; rpt. London: Cambridge University Press, 1971), p. 103.

6. The dispute over how Muhamad Muhashamy raised his daughter and "paraded" his wife around revealed the tension over the question of a father's and husband's authority within the family. A Muslim wife was to be obedient to her husband, and a daughter to her father. But the family of a man's wife retained an interest in, if not authority over, her behavior. For obedience to one's husband see the nineteenth-century poem, Alice Werner and William Hichens, eds., *Utendi wa Mwana Kupona (Advice of Mwana Kupona upon the Wifely Duty)*, The Azanian Classics, vol. 2 (Medstead: Azania Press, 1934). Based on research in the mid 1970s in Mombasa, Marc J. Swarz found agreement from both women and men that men should have and do have the power to control a wife's behavior; "The Isolation of Men and the Happiness of Women: Sources and Uses of Power in Swahili Marital Relationships," *Journal of Anthropological Research* 38 (1982), 26-44; and "Culture and Implicit Power: Maneuvers and Understandings in Swahili Nuclear Family Relationships," in *Culture and Political Change*, ed. Myron J. Aronoff (New Brunswick, N.J.: Transaction Books, 1983), pp. 19-38. For a discussion of the Muslim elite's fears of the breakdown of parental authority, see Margaret Strobel, *Muslim Women in Mombasa, 1890-1975* (New Haven and London: Yale University Press, 1979), p. 96.

7. Nowadays many parents delay a girl's donning the *buibui* until she completes her schooling, although under the influence of Islamic fundamentalism some girls put on the veil before completion. In the 1970s it was extremely uncommon for a grown

woman to be seen on the streets of Mombasa without a *buibui*.

8. Eighty percent of women age 55 and over in Mombasa never attended school, according to figures from the 1979 census. Mwana Kutani is among the 17% who "left school." The numbers are 4,772 "never attended" and 1,020 "left school" out of a total of 5,949 women 55 years old and over. The remaining 3% are in the categories "at school" and "not stated." Kenya, Central Bureau of Statistics, Ministry of Economic Planning and Development, *Kenya Population Census 1979*, Vol. I (Nairobi: [Government Printer], June 1981), p. 240, Table 4. However, the percentage of women of Mwana Kutani's age with some education is higher for Mombasa as a whole than within her own community because it includes the non-Muslim population that is more likely to have attended mission school. A better sense can be gained from the 1931 census of "non-natives," which would include Arabs, Asians, and Europeans. Here only 3% of non-native girls were in school and 2% were receiving private instruction, compared with 9% in school and 3% receiving private instruction for boys. Kenya Colony and Protectorate, *Report of the Non-native Census, 6 March 1931* (Nairobi: Government Printer, 1932) p. 130, Table 32. This census may underreport older women who were literate in Arabic or in Swahili in Arabic script. At the time of the interviews Mwana Kutani was literate in Swahili, could read and speak some English, and was teaching herself to read Arabic.

For Arab or Swahili parents interested in educating their daughters, there were few options in the late 1920s and early 1930s. A girls' school had been founded in Zanzibar in 1927. But the Ghazali Private Muslim School in Mombasa that Bi Kaje mentions, which became the Arab Girls' School, was not founded until the mid-1930s. Zanzibar Education Department, "The Arab Girls' School of Zanzibar," *Oversea Education* 1, no. 4 (July 1930), 125-30. For girls' education in Mombasa, see Strobel, *Muslim Women*, pp. 106-13.

9. Fatma Husein suggests that there might have been religious and language differences at play. Goan Catholic schools would not have accepted Hindu or Muslim children. In Zanzibar, Asian schools used Gujerati as the language of instruction; Hindu schools did not admit Muslims; Ismaili schools did not admit Ithnashari Muslims, even though both are Shia. (Private communication, 3-30-88.)

10. The gravity of Shamsa's parents' decision to enroll her at the Church Missionary Society's Buxton School can be seen in the commentary, published a year after they withdrew her, from Sheik Al-Amin bin Ali Mazrui. In his Swahili newspaper *Al-Islah* [Reform], he argued for the establishment of Muslim education for girls. Without it, he charged,

> we will be aiding our girls to join the mission school, where most students come to read. And those poor people do not know that they have put their children in HELL, for

missions do not open schools except to trap Muslims into
becoming Christians. To send a child to [mission] school is
the worst sort of crime.
"Taalim ya Vijana Wanawake" [Education of young girls],
Uwongozi [Guidance] (ca. 1932; rpt. Mombasa: East African
Muslim Welfare Society, 1955), essay no. 3 (1931), p. 4. Our
translation. Sheik Al-Amin bin Ali Mazrui's essays have been
reprinted in the pamphlet *Uwongozi*, which was still for sale in the
1970s in Mombasa bookstores.
    11. High administrative positions were reserved for Europeans,
except those who interpreted Muslim law, e.g., the Liwali and
Mudirs.
    12. Note the use of *somo* instead of *kungwi*, which elites
associated with slave/ex-slave culture.
    13. This statement suggests she spent the early years of her
marriage in a closer relationship with her husband than with a
community of women, since attending weddings and funerals is a
major activity done by married women with other women.
    14. She could not divorce her husband, since the Shafi'i school of
Muslim personal law followed on the Coast limits a woman's right
to initiate divorce to such causes as a husband's impotence, serious
disease, or failure to maintain the wife at the standard of living
agreed upon at marriage. So, Mwana Kutani followed the common
strategy of provoking him until he divorced her.
    15. Her negotiations with her second husband prior to their
marriage indicate the freedom a woman had in selecting mates
following her first marriage, although in this case her father's
death may have contributed to her autonomy.
    16. She is referring to her sometimes raucous *lelemama*
activities.
    17. This passage suggests the difficulty of remaining unmarried,
particularly for someone in her thirties and as involved in public
activities as Mwana Kutani. See also Gill Shepherd, "Rank,
Gender, and Homosexuality: Mombasa as a Key to Understanding
Sexual Options," in *The Cultural Construction of Sexuality*, ed. Pat
Caplan (London and New York: Tavistock Publications, 1987),
240-70.

My Work in Women's Organizations

    1. Her account emphasizes the various procedures in the
marketing of *leso*, or *kanga* as they were also called, that they were
protesting. In contrast, Bi Kaje, in discussions not included here,
showed little recollection of the detailed purpose of the boycott but
vividly recalled the disunity it revealed among Swahili people. The
increase in prices that in part provoked the boycott may have
reflected wartime inflation as much as the exploitation of Indian
merchants. Hyder Kindy, *Life and Politics in Mombasa* (Nairobi:
East African Publishing House, 1972), p. 109.

2. Frederick Cooper questioned whether Japan was exporting textiles to this area at this time. Sharifa Zawawi, who has studied *kunga*, says they did, and that Japanese cloth was considered inferior. (Personal communication in comments on the manuscript.)

3. Since the mid 1970s people have reduced the scale of and expenditures on weddings considerably out of economic necessity.

4. In conversation, people call Ibinaal Watan "Ibinaa."

5 Mwana Kutani's account of the *lelemama* competition stresses the way she and her friends in Banu Saada and Ibinaal Watan broke with traditions by dancing publicly, unveiled. Even though her socialization had been unconventional, she herself was, upon reflection, shocked by her activities. Yet after the fuss died down, the liberating effect of having defied convention remained. Mwana Kutani, like virtually all Arab and Swahili women in Mombasa, still wears a *buibui*. But in other ways her lifestyle differs significantly from that of women of Bi Kaje's generation.

6. This organization's name was only in English; there was no Swahili version. Although there is no evidence of European women's involvement in the Muslim Women's Institute, European women initiated Women's Institutes in various British colonies in the 1940s and 1950s; Joan Alexander, *Voices and Echoes: Tales from Colonial Women* (London: Quartet Books, 1983), pp. 141-51; Deborah Kirkwood, "Settler Wives in Rhodesia: A Case Study," in *The Incorporated Wife*, ed. Hillary Callan and Shirley Ardener (London: Croom Helm, 1984), pp. 143-64; Audrey Wipper, "The Maendeleo ya Wanawake Movement in the Colonial Period: The Canadian Connection, Mau Mau, Embroidery and Agriculture," *Rural Africana* No. 29 (Winter 1975-76), 195-214.

7. A special dish made of rice, onions, lamb (or chicken), saffron, and other spices.

8. Mwana Kutani has worked hard to raise funds for the Institute to build a hall, which was finally begun in 1976. Like others, she views the Arab and Swahili community in competition with Indians. In comparing, she finds that her own people lack the unity and education characteristic of the Indian community.

9. Titles and roles that derived from English words and Western roles replaced the former Swahili/Arabic titles and the queens, dukes, and ladies of the later *lelemama* groups.

10. The formation of the Arab Women's Institute was announced in the *Mombasa Times* on December 19, 1957.

11. As is commonly the case, Mwana Kutani was asked to mobilize the women's vote for a campaign that did not raise women's issues. Instead, the men sought to gain the women's vote for the goals the men had established.

12. Examinations prepared in Cambridge University that mark the end of secondary school. "O Levels" (ordinary level) are taken after the equivalent of eleventh grade in the United States. "A Levels" (advanced level) are taken at the completion of thirteen years of education, i.e., one year more than U.S. high school. As of

1985, Kenyan students do eight years of primary school, four years of secondary school, and four years of university.

13. The Kenya African Democratic Union (KADU) and the Kenya African National Union (KANU). For details on the political context, see Cherry Gertzel, *The Politics of Independent Kenya, 1963-1968* (Nairobi: East African Publishing House, 1970), and A. I. Salim, *The Swahili-Speaking Peoples of Kenya's Coast, 1895-1965* (Nairobi: East African Publishing House, 1973).

14. Women's Progress, the national women's organization. See Audrey Wipper, "The Maendeleo ya Wanawake Movement: Some Paradoxes and Contradictions," *African Studies Review* 18, no. 3 (December 1975), 99-120.

15. The equivalent of grades 1-4 in the United States.

16. This portion of the interview was conducted in 1975, which the United Nations declared to be International Women's Year. It was honored by the printing of a special *kanga*.

17. The Muslim Women's Cultural Association was formed after the Muslim Women's Institute by women who felt that the former was elitist. The rivalry between these organizations fits the pattern of the rivalry between *lelemama* groups and between groups of *makungwi*. See Strobel, *Muslim Women*, Chapter 7.

18. Shamsa Muhashamy's point is that women these days spend less time visiting and more time doing their own work, an observation shared by Sarah Mirza.

Appendix

1. Derek Nurse and Thomas Spear, *The Swahili: Reconstructing the History and Language of an African Society* (Philadelphia: University of Pennsylvania Press, 1985), p. 32.

2. Thomas Hinnebusch and Sarah Mirza, *Kiswahili: A Foundation for Speaking, Reading, and Writing* (Washington, D.C.: University Press of America, 1979), p. xiv.

3. Nurse and Spear, p. 49.

4. Nurse and Spear, pp. 32-34.

5. Nurse and Spear, pp. 46-51.

6. (1939; rpt. London: Oxford University Press, 1967).

7. (2nd ed., 1882; rpt. London: Gregg Press, 1964).

8. Wilfred Whitely, *Swahili: The Rise of a National Language*, Studies in African History, 3 (London: Methuen, 1969), Chapter 1.

9. Whitely, Chapter 4.

10. Whitely, Chapter 5, and Joan Russell, *Communicative Competence in a Minority Community: A Sociolinguistic Study of the Swahili-Speaking Community in the Old Town, Mombasa* (Leiden: Brill, 1981).

REFERENCES

We have not found an entirely satisfactory way of alphabetizing Muslim names. In the following bibliography, most Muslim authors of books in English are listed under their last names, which is how the reader is most likely to find them in a card catalog. Some Muslim authors in English whose last names are not so clearly surnames in the English manner and those who write in Swahili are alphabetized by their first names.

Archives

Land Office, Mombasa. Collected by Frederick Cooper, Karim Janmohamed, and John Zarwan
Kenya National Archives, Jogoo House, Nairobi. Coast Deposit 1

Official Documents

Kenya, Ministry of Finance and Economic Planning, Statistical Division. *Kenya Population Census 1969*, Vol. III. Nairobi: Government Printer, 1970.
Kenya, Central Bureau of Statistics, Ministry of Economic Planning and Development. *Kenya Population Census 1979*, Vol. I. Nairobi: [Government Printer], June 1981.
Kenya Colony and Protectorate. *Report of the Non-native Census, 6 March 1931*. Nairobi: Government Printer, 1932.

Unpublished Dissertations and Typescripts

Berg, James. "Mombasa under the Busaidi Sultanate: The City and Its Hinterland in the Nineteenth Century." Ph.D. dissertation, University of Wisconsin, 1971.
Biersteker, Ann. "The Seductive Power of Language/The Power of Seductive Language: A Reconsideration of "Utendi wa Mwana Kupona." Paper presented at the African Studies Association conference, 1987.
Franken, Marjorie Ann. "Anyone Can Dance: A Survey and

Analysis of Swahili Ngoma, Past and Present." Ph.D. dissertation, University of California, Riverside, 1986.
Giles, Linda Lavinia. "Spirit Possession on the Swahili Coast." Ph.D. dissertation, University of Texas, Austin, forthcoming.
Mbilinyi, Marjorie. "Politics of Personal Narratives." Paper presented at conference on "Autobiographies, Biographies and Life Histories of Women: Interdisciplinary Perspectives," University of Minnesota, May 23-24, 1986.
Shostak, Marjorie. "What the Wind Won't Take Away: Methodologies and Ethical Considerations of the Oral History of a Hunting-Gathering Woman." Paper presented at conference on "Autobiographies, Biographies and Life Histories of Women: Interdisciplinary Perspectives," University of Minnesota, May 23-24, 1986.
Topan, Farouk Mohamedhussein Tharia. "Oral Literature in a Ritual Setting: The Role of Spirit Songs in a Spirit-Mediumship Cult of Mombasa, Kenya." Ph.D. dissertation, University of London, 1971.
Wright, Marcia. "Since 'Women in Peril': Reconsiderations of Biography, Autobiography and Life Stories of Some African Women with Special Reference to Marriage." Paper presented at conference on "Autobiographies, Biographies and Life Histories of Women: Interdisciplinary Perspectives," University of Minnesota, May 23-24, 1986.
Zawawi, Sharifa. "Cloth and the Message in East Africa." Paper presented at African Studies Association conference, 1987.

Newspaper

Mombasa Times

Published Books and Articles

Alexander, Joan. *Voices and Echoes: Tales from Colonial Women.* London: Quartet Books, 1983.
Allen, James de Vere. "The 'Shirazi' Problem in East African Coastal History." *Paideuma* 28 (1982), 9-27.
____. "Swahili Culture Reconsidered: Some Historical Implications of the Material Culture of the Northern Kenya Coast in the Eighteenth and Nineteeth Centuries." *Azania* 9 (1974), 105-37.
____. "Town and Country in Swahili Culture." In *Perspectives des Études Africaines Contemporaines,* pp. 298-316. Cologne: Deutsche UNESCO-Kommission, 1974.
Alpers, Edward A. *Ivory and Slaves: Changing Patterns of International Trade to the Late Nineteenth Century.* Berkeley and Los Angeles: University of California Press, 1975.
____. "The Story of Swema: Female Vulnerability in Nineteenth-Century East Africa." In *Women and Slavery in Africa,* ed. Claire C. Robertson and Martin A. Klein, pp. 185-219. Madison:

University of Wisconsin Press, 1983.
Amiji, Hakim. "The Bohoras of East Africa." *Journal of Religion in Africa* (1976), 27-40.
Al-Amin bin Ali Mazrui, Sheik. "Ada Zetu Maarusini" [Our wedding customs], essay no. 13, p. 23. In *Uwongozi*, [Guidance]. Ca. 1932. Reprint, Mombasa: East African Muslim Welfare Society, 1955.
_____. "Taalim ya Vijana Wanawake" [Education of young girls], essay no. 3 (1931), p. 4. In *Uwongozi* [Guidance]. Ca. 1932. Reprint, Mombasa: East African Muslim Welfare Society, 1955.
Bennett, Norman R. "The Church Missionary Society at Mombasa, 1873-1894." *Boston University Papers in African History* 1 (1964), 159-95.
Berg, F. J. "The Coast from the Portuguese Invasion to the Rise of the Zanzibar Sultanate." In *Zamani: A Survey of East African History*, ed. B. A. Ogot, pp. 115-34. 2nd ed. Nairobi: East African Publishing House, 1973. (1st ed., 1968)
_____. "The Swahili Community of Mombasa, 1500-1900." *Journal of African History* 9, no. 1 (1968), 35-56.
Berg, F. J., and B. J. Walter. "Mosques, Population and Urban Development in Mombasa." *Hadith 1* (1968), 47-100.
Busaidy, Hamed bin Saleh El-. *Ndoa na Talaka* [Marriage and divorce]. Nairobi: East African Literature Bureau, 1958.
Campbell, Carol A., and Carol M. Eastman. *"Ngoma:* Swahili Adult Song Performance in Context." *Ethnomusicology* 28, no. 3 (September 1984), 467-93.
Caplan, A. P. "Boys' Circumcision and Girls' Puberty Rites among the Swahili of Mafia Island." *Africa* 46, no. 1 (1976), 21-33.
Caplan, Pat. "Gender, Ideology and Modes of Production on the Coast of East Africa." *Paideuma* 28 (1982), 29-43.
Chittick, H. Neville. "The Coast before the Arrival of the Portuguese." In *Zamani: A Survey of East African History*, ed. B. A. Ogot, pp. 98-114. 2nd ed. Nairobi: East African Publishing House, 1973. (1st ed., 1968)
_____. "The Shirazi Colonization of East Africa." *Journal of African History* 6, no. 3 (1965), 275-94.
Cooper, Frederick. *From Slaves to Squatters: Plantation Labor and Agriculture in Zanzibar and Coastal Kenya, 1980-1925.* New Haven and London: Yale University Press, 1980.
_____. *Plantation Slavery on the East Coast of Africa.* New Haven and London: Yale University Press, 1977.
Curtin, Patricia Romero. "Laboratory for the Oral History of Slavery: The Island of Lamu on the Kenya Coast." *American Historical Review* 88, no. 4 (October 1983), 858-82.
_____. "Weddings in Lamu, Kenya: An Example of Social and Economic Change." *Cahiers d'Études Africaines* 24, no. 2 (1984), 131-55.
Donley, Linda Wiley. "House Power: Swahili Space and Symbolic Markers." In *Symbolic and Structural Archaeology*, ed. Ian

Hodder, pp. 63-73. Cambridge: Cambridge University Press, 1982.

Emecheta, Buchi. *The Joy of Motherhood.* New York: George Braziller, 1979.

Fabian, Johannes. *Language and Colonial Power: The Appropriation of Swahili in the Former Belgian Congo, 1880-1938.* African Studies Series, no. 48. New York: Cambridge University Press, 1986.

Frontiers: A Journal of Women's Studies 7, no. 1 (1983).

Geiger, Susan N. G. "Women's Life Histories: Method and Content." *Signs* 11, no. 2 (1986), 334-51.

Gertzel, Cherry. *The Politics of Independent Kenya, 1963-1968.* Nairobi: East African Publishing House, 1970.

Giles, Linda Lavinia. "Possession Cults on the Swahili Coast: A Re-examination of Theories of Marginality." *Africa* 57, no. 2 (1987), 234-58.

Gray, John Milner. *"Nairuz or Siku ya Mwaka."* *Tanganyika Notes and Records* 38 (1955), 1-22.

Hansen, Karen Tranberg. *Distant Companions: Servants and Employers in Zambia, 1900-1985.* Ithaca, N.Y.: Cornell University Press, 1989.

Hinawiy, Mbarak bin Ali. "Notes on Customs in Mombasa." *Swahili* 34, pt. 1 (1964), 17-35.

Hinnebusch, Thomas, and Sarah Mirza. *Kiswahili: A Foundation for Speaking, Reading, and Writing.* Washington, D.C.: University Press of America, 1979.

Hodges, Geoffrey. *The Carrier Corps: Military Labor in the East African Campaign, 1914-1918.* Westport, Conn.: Greenwood Press, 1986.

Hourani, Albert. *Arabic Thought in the Liberal Age, 1798-1939.* London: Oxford University Press, 1962.

Hyder Kindy. *Life and Politics in Mombasa.* Nairobi: East African Publishing House, 1972.

Janmohamed, Karim. "African Laborers in Mombasa, c. 1895-1940." *Hadith 5, Economic and Social History of Africa* (1975), pp. 154-76.

Johnson, Frederick. *A Standard Swahili-English Dictionary.* 1939. Reprint, London: Oxford University Press, 1967.

Kirkwood, Deborah. "Settler Wives in Rhodesia: A Case Study." In *The Incorporated Wife,* ed. Hillary Callan and Shirley Ardener, pp. 143-64. London: Croom Helm, 1984.

Kluckhohn, Clyde. "The Personal Document in Anthropological Science." In *The Use of Personal Documents in History, Anthropology and Sociology,* by Louis Gottschalk, Clyde Kluckhohn, and Robert Angell, Bulletin 53, pp. 77-173. New York: Social Science Research Council, 1945.

Krapf, Ludwig. *A Dictionary of the Suahili Language.* 2nd ed. London: Gregg Press, 1964. (1st ed., 1882)

Lambek, Michael. *Human Spirits: A Cultural Account of Trance in*

Mayotte. Cambridge and New York: Cambridge University Press, 1981.

Langness, L. L., and Gelya Frank. *Lives: An Anthropological Approach to Biography.* Novato, Calif.: Chandler and Sharp Publishers, Inc., 1981.

Levy, Reuben. *The Social Structure of Islam: Being the Second Edition of the Sociology of Islam.* 1957. Reprint, London: Cambridge University Press, 1971.

Lienhardt, Peter. "Introduction." In *The Medicine Man, Swifa ya Nguvumali,* by Hasani bin Ismail, ed. and trans. Peter Lienhardt. London: Oxford University Press, 1968.

Mbotela, James. *The Freeing of the Slaves.* London: Evans Brothers, 1956.

Meillassoux, Claude. "Female Slavery." In *Women and Slavery in Africa,* ed. Claire C. Robertson and Martin A. Klein, pp. 49-66. Madison: University of Wisconsin Press, 1983.

Mirza, Sarah, and Margaret Strobel. "The Life History of Mishi wa Abdala, a Swahili Kungwi of Mombasa, Kenya." *The African Review* 11, no. 1 (1984), 68-80.

Morton, R. F. "The Shungwaya Myth of Miji Kenda Origins: A Problem of Nineteenth Century Kenya Coastal History." *African Historical Studies* 5, no. 3 (1972), 397-423.

Mtoro bin Mwinyi Bakari. *The Customs of the Swahili People: The Desturi za Waswahili of Mtoro bin Mwinyi Bakari and Other Swahili Persons,* ed. and trans. J. W. T. Allen. Berkeley: University of California Press, 1981.

Nichols, C. S. *The Swahili Coast: Politics, Diplomacy and Trade on the East African Littoral, 1798-1856.* St. Anthony's College, Oxford, Publications no. 2. London: George Allen and Unwin, 1971.

Nurse, Derek, and Thomas Spear. *The Swahili: Reconstructing the History and Language of an African Society.* Philadelphia: University of Pennsylvania Press, 1985.

Personal Narratives Group. *Interpreting Women's Lives: Feminist Theory and Personal Narrative.* Bloomington: Indiana University Press, forthcoming.

Pouwels, Randall L. "Sh. Al-Amin b. Ali Mazrui and Islamic Modernism in East Africa, 1875-1947." *International Journal of Middle Eastern Studies* 13 (1981), pp. 329-45.

Ranger, T. O. *Dance and Society in Eastern Africa, 1890-1970: The Beni Ngoma.* Berkeley: University of California Press, 1975.

———. "Missionary Adaptation of African Religious Institutions: The Masasi Case." In *The Historical Study of African Religion,* ed. T. O. Ranger and Isaria Kimambo, pp. 221-51. London: Heinemann, 1972.

Reichard, Paul. *Deutsch-Ostafrika: Das Land und Seine Bewohner.* Leipzig: Otto Spamer, 1892.

Robertson, Claire C., and Martin A. Klein. "Women's Importance in African Slave Systems." In *Women and Slavery in Africa,* ed.

Claire C. Robertson and Martin A. Klein, pp. 3-25. Madison: University of Wisconsin Press, 1983.

Rollins, Jack D. *A History of Swahili Prose: Part One: From Earliest Times to the End of the Nineteenth Century.* Leiden: E.J. Brill, 1983.

Romero, Patricia W., ed. *Life Histories of African Women.* London and Atlantic Highlands, N. J.: Ashfield Press, 1987.

_____. "Mama Khadija." In *Life Histories of African Women,* ed. Patricia W. Romero, pp. 140-58. London and Atlantic Highlands, N.J.: The Ashfield Press, 1987.

_____. "'Where Have All the Slaves Gone?': Emancipation and Post-emancipation in Lamu, Kenya." *Journal of African History* 27, no. 3 (1986), 497-512.

Russell, Joan. *Communicative Competence in a Minority Community: A Sociolinguistic Study of the Swahili-Speaking Community in the Old Town, Mombasa.* Leiden: Brill, 1981.

Sacleux, Charles. *Dictionnaire Swahili-Française.* Travaux et Memoires de l'Institut d'Ethnologie, vols. 36 and 37. Paris: Institut d'Ethnologie, 1939.

Salim, A. I. "Sir Ali Bin Salim." *Kenya Historical Biographies,* ed. A. I. Salim and Kenneth King, pp. 112-41. Nairobi Historical Studies, No. 2. Nairobi: University of Nairobi, 1971.

_____. *The Swahili-Speaking Peoples of Kenya's Coast, 1895-1965.* Nairobi: East African Publishing House, 1973.

Shepherd, Gill. "Rank, Gender, and Homosexuality: Mombasa as a Key to Understanding Sexual Options." In *The Cultural Construction of Sexuality,* ed. Pat Caplan, pp. 240-70. London and New York: Tavistock Publications, 1987.

_____. "Two Marriage Forms in the Comoro Islands: An Investigation." *Africa* 47, no. 4 (1977), 344-59.

Shostak, Marjorie. *Nisa: The Life and Words of a !Kung Woman.* Cambridge: Harvard University Press, 1981.

Silberman, Leo. "The Social Survey of the Old Town of Mombasa." *Journal of African Administration* 2 (January 1950), 14-21.

Smith, Mary F. *Baba of Karo: A Woman of the Muslim Hausa.* 1954. Reprint, New Haven and London: Yale University Press, 1981.

Smith, M. G. "Introduction." In *Baba of Karo: A Woman of the Muslim Hausa,* by Mary F. Smith. 1954. Reprint, New Haven: Yale University Press, 1981.

Spear, Thomas. *Traditions of Origin and Their Interpretation: The Mijikenda of Kenya.* Athens: Ohio University Press, 1982.

Steere, Edward. *Swahili Tales, as Told by the Natives of Zanzibar.* London: Bell and Daldy, 1870.

Stigand, Capt. C. H. *The Land of the Zinj.* London: Constable and Co., 1913.

Strobel, Margaret. "Doing Oral History as an Outsider." *Frontiers: A Journal of Women's Studies* 2, no. 2 (1977), 68-72.

_____. "Gender and Race in the Nineteenth- and Twentieth-Century

British Empire." In *Becoming Visible: Women in European History*, ed. Renate Bridenthal, Claudia Koonz, and Susan Stuard, pp. 375-96. New York: Houghton Mifflin, 1987.

———. *Muslim Women in Mombasa, 1890-1975*. New Haven and London: Yale University Press, 1979.

———. "Slavery and Reproductive Labor in Mombasa." In *Women and Slavery in Africa*, ed. Claire C. Robertson and Martin A. Klein, pp. 111-29. Madison: University of Wisconsin Press, 1983.

Swartz, Marc J. "Culture and Implicit Power: Maneuvers and Understandings in Swahili Nuclear Family Relations." In *Culture and Political Change*, ed. Myron J. Aronoff, pp. 19-38. New Brunswick, N.J.: Transaction Books, 1983.

———. "The Isolation of Men and the Happiness of Women: Sources and Use of Power in Swahili Marital Relationships." *Journal of Anthropological Research* 38 (1982), 26-44.

Tanner, R. E. S., and D. F. Roberts. "A Demographic Study in an Area of Low Fertility in North-east Tanganyika." *Population Studies* 13 (1959-60), 61-80.

Theisz, R. D. "The Critical Collaboration: Introductions as a Gateway to the Study of Native American Bi-Autobiography." *American Indian Culture and Research Journal* 5, no. 1 (1981), 65-80.

Turner, Victor. *The Drums of Affliction: A Study of Religious Processes among the Ndembu of Zambia*. Oxford: Clarendon Press, 1968.

———. *The Forest of Symbols: Aspects of Ndembu Ritual*. Ithaca, N.Y.: Cornell University Press, 1967.

———. *The Ritual Process: Structure and Anti-structure*. London: Routledge and Kegan Paul, 1969.

Watson, Lawrence C. "Understanding a Life History as a Subjective Document: Hermeneutical and Phenomenological Perspectives." *Ethos* 4, no. 1 (Spring 1976), 95-131.

Werner, Alice, and William Hichens, eds. *Utendi wa Mwana Kupona (Advice of Mwana Kupona upon the Wifely Duty)*. The Azanian Classics, vol. 2. Medstead: Azania Press, 1934.

Whitely, Wilfred. *Swahili: The Rise of a National Language*. Studies in African History, 3. London: Methuen, 1969.

Wipper, Audrey. "The Maendeleo ya Wanawake Movement: Some Paradoxes and Contradictions." *African Studies Review* 18, no. 3 (December 1975), 99-120.

———. "The Maendeleo ya Wanawake Movement in the Colonial Period: The Canadian Connection, Mau Mau, Embroidery and Agriculture." *Rural Africana* no. 29 (Winter 1975-76), 195-214.

Wright, Marcia. "Women in Peril: A Commentary on the Life Stories of Captives in Nineteenth-Century East-Central Africa." *African Social Research* 20 (1975), 800-19.

———. *Women in Peril*. Lusaka: NECZAM, 1984.

Wrye, Harriet, and Jacqueline Churcilla. "Looking Inward, Looking Backward: Reminiscence and the Life Review." *Frontiers: A*

Journal of Women's Studies 2, no. 2 (1977), 98-105.
Zanzibar Education Department. "The Arab Girls' School of Zanzibar." *Oversea Education* 1, no. 4 (July 1930), 125-30.
Zawawi, Sharifa. *Contact and Change: A Study of the East African Coast.* Great Neck, N.Y.: Todd and Honeywell, forthcoming.
Zein, Abdul Hamid el-. *The Sacred Meadows: A Structural Analysis of Religion Symbolism in an East African Town.* Evanston, Ill.: Northwestern University Press, 1974.

INDEX

Swahili and Arab names have been alphabetized by the first letter of their name as it is found in the text, even where this word might be read by a Swahili-speaker as a title.